THE INTERN TEACHER CASEBOOK

July 1988

Teacher Trainees
Leila Brandt
Linda Dmytriw
Christine E. Emmel
Anthony C. Gargano
Michael A. Miller
William A. Rossbach

John Shearer
Eric A. Steinberg
Vickie P. White

Experienced Teachers
Donna Colbert
Karen Desser
Don Kemper

Joel Littauer
Patricia Norton
Gerald A. Richer
Susan Taira

*Teacher Educator/
Educational Scholars*
Jere Brophy

Michigan State
University
Pam Grossman
University of
Washington
Lee S. Shulman
Stanford University

Edited by

Judith H. Shulman
Far West Laboratory for
Educational Research and Development

Joel A. Colbert
Los Angeles Unified School District
California State University, Dominguez Hills

Published by
Far West Laboratory for Educational Research and Development
and
ERIC Clearinghouse on Educational Management
and
ERIC Clearinghouse on Teacher Education

International Standard Book Number: 0-86552-095-X
Library of Congress Catalog Card Number: 88-81826

Printed in the United States of America
ERIC Clearinghouse on Educational Management
University of Oregon, Eugene, Oregon 97403
and
Far West Laboratory for Educational Research and
Development
1855 Folsom Street, San Francisco, California 94103
and
ERIC Clearinghouse on Teacher Education
American Association of Colleges for Teacher Education
One Dupont Circle, Suite 610
Washington, DC 20036

No federal funds were used in the printing of this publication

The University of Oregon, the Far West Laboratory, and the American Association of
Colleges for Teacher Education are affirmative action, equal opportunity institutions.

B2866

This document is published jointly by the Far West
Laboratory for Educational Research and Development,
the ERIC Clearinghouse on Educational Management,
and the ERIC Clearinghouse on Teacher Education. The
research at the Far West Laboratory was supported by
federal funds from the U.S. Department of Education,
Office of Educational Research and Improvement,
contract number 400-86-0009. The contents of this
publication do not necessarily reflect the views or policies
of the Department of Education nor does mention of trade
names, commercial products or organizations imply
endorsement by the United States Government.
Reprint rights are granted with proper credit.

About FWL

Far West Laboratory for Educational Research and Development is located in San Francisco. With primary funding from the U.S. Department of Education, it conducts research, provides technical assistance and training, and offers evaluation support to schools and education agencies. In addition, for 22 years, FWL has been a federally designated regional laboratory with the charge to provide service and support for the public schools in Arizona, California, Nevada and Utah. Other funding comes from state and private sources, and addresses the entire range of educational concerns—from pre-school experiences through adult literacy.

About ERIC

The Educational Resources Information Center (ERIC) is a national information system operated by the U.S. Department of Education. The ERIC Clearinghouse on Educational Management was established at the University of Oregon in 1966. The ERIC Clearinghouse on Teacher Education has been operated by the American Association of Colleges for Teacher Education since June 1968. ERIC serves the education community by disseminating research results and other resource information that can be used in developing more effective educational programs. Research results and journal articles are announced regularly in ERIC's index and abstract bulletins.

Besides processing documents and journal articles, the Clearinghouses prepare bibliographies, literature reviews, monographs, and other interpretive research studies on topics in their educational areas.

FOREWORD

The Far West Laboratory for Educational Research and Development, the ERIC Clearinghouse on Educational Management, and the ERIC Clearinghouse on Teacher Education are pleased to make this publication available to their respective clienteles. The Far West Laboratory has a rich history of helping chart new paths in education, while the Clearinghouses are committed to disseminating information useful for the operation and improvement of elementary and secondary schools.

The Intern Teacher Casebook is an example of the Laboratory's commitment to building and using practitioner knowledge. In partnership with the Los Angeles Unified School District, FWL developed real-life vignettes for role playing and case study activities in workshops for training beginning teachers. As a training document, this volume works well. At the same time, the content of the vignettes yields a goldmine of information on the types of help new and beginning teachers need and want.

Presenting the vignettes and training discussions in a casebook format is an additional contribution of this volume. There is too little room for teachers' own voices in materials used to train them. The practical knowledge and insight that years of experience provide are often used to train new professionals in fields other than education. This volume confronts that void with humor, pathos and know-how— indeed, with the very qualities that go into truly fine teaching.

Dean H. Nafziger
Director
Far West Laboratory
for Educational Research
and Development

Philip K. Piele
Director
ERIC Clearinghouse on
Educational Management

Mary E. Dilworth
Director
ERIC Clearinghouse on
Teacher Education

TABLE OF CONTENTS

PREFACE

This volume is the second in a series of Close-to-the-Classroom Casebooks, published by the Far West Laboratory for Educational Research and Development (FWL), as part of the Effective Support for Beginning Teachers Program. The casebook was developed collaboratively by a researcher from FWL, a staff developer/ researcher from the Los Angeles Unified School District (LAUSD), and nine teacher trainees from the district.

Teacher trainees are secondary teachers with a bachelor's degree in a subject area, who are enrolled in a teacher preparation program conducted by the district. The book contains cases on selected first-year experiences, written by the trainees themselves. The problems described are similar to those that any novice might face during the first year of teaching in a school located in a large metropolitan area.

These Close-to-the-Classroom Casebooks are part of a larger effort to build and use practitioner knowledge in teaching and teacher education. While research-based knowledge of the teaching experience has grown in volume and usefulness, practitioner analyses remain a relatively small part of a teacher's information about teaching and learning. The profession has few mechanisms to record and preserve a particular teacher's accumulated knowledge about teaching. When teachers retire or otherwise leave teaching, their understanding, methods, and materials which should form a legacy to the profession, the community, and the school are generally lost. By combining research and practitioner knowledge, the Close-to-the-Classroom Casebooks contribute to the growing body of case literature on the practitioner experience.

What do we mean by a "case"? A case is not simply any narrative account of an event. To call something a case is to make a theoretical claim — that it is a "case of something," or an instance of a larger class (L. Shulman, 1986). For example, an account of a teacher observing a colleague teach a lesson and later engaging that colleague in an analysis of the lesson is a case of coaching. Cases may also be exemplars of principles, describing by their detail a general pattern of practice.

All the narratives (or vignettes, as we often call them) included in this casebook meet this criterion. They have been selected because they are representative of a larger class of experiences. They are, in that sense, cases.

The cases presented in this book are written by newcomers to the profession, about an event or sequence of events during their first year of teaching. The cases describe the circumstances of each event, its consequences, and the ongoing thoughts and feelings of the participants. Unlike case studies, which are analytical documents written by outside observers or researchers, these vignettes are personal, descriptive accounts of problems that the novices themselves face as they struggle to survive their first few months of teaching. Most of the vignettes are accompanied by reactions from other teachers and educational scholars to give a multiple perspective of the situation described. Cases in the first two chapters are grouped by problems relating to instructional events and interactions with students. A third chapter focuses on interactions with other teachers who influenced the newcomers' teaching methods.

Background

The casebook series draws from Far West Laboratory's two-year study of first year implementation of the California Mentor Teacher Program. At the end of this project, Shulman used selected research-based vignettes about teachers' interactions with mentor teachers during inservice activities with local mentor teachers, staff developers, and district administrators. She discovered that the vignettes served as a powerful catalyst to stimulate discussion about issues concerning the new role of mentor teachers. Participants in the workshops reacted to the vignettes, shared personal experiences, discussed common problems, and deliberated about new ways of asserting the mentorship. Reacting to stories about other mentors' experiences made it easier for some participants to talk about their own. As one mentor coordinator said, "The vignettes stimulated our staff to discuss issues that were heretofore buried under the table."

This experience guided the planning of a new project — a casebook from the mentor teachers' perspective, using vignettes written by the mentors themselves. We believed that, given proper preparation and support, we could provide the opportunity for experienced teachers to contribute to the growing case literature on teaching, heretofore dominated by researchers.

The Mentor Teacher Casebook (Shulman and Colbert, 1986) represents the Laboratory's first attempt to develop a case literature of teaching. These cases — narrative vignettes written by 22 practicing mentor teachers in the Los Angeles Unified School District about their work providing on-the-job assistance to beginning teachers — highlight issues that reflect the complexity of asserting the new mentor role. Selected accounts are accompanied by commentary by other mentors. The vignettes were written during a course in staff development for mentor teachers taught by Colbert. At the end of the class, the mentors unanimously agreed that writing vignettes was an excellent staff development technique. They reported that the cases stimulated reflective analysis of their own skills and provided a catalyst for interaction with their colleagues about their concerns regarding the mentor role.

The current volume serves as a partner to *The Mentor Teacher Casebook*. It provides a window to the first-year experience for all experienced teachers who are engaged in helping newcomers into the profession.

Acknowledgements

We would like to thank the staff of the Los Angeles Unified School District for having the courage to support the portrayal of candid first-year experiences of some of their new teachers. In particular, Bob DeVries and Norm Marks at the Human Resources Development Branch and Paul Possemato, Associate Superintendent of the Policy Implementation and Evaluation Unit, provided astute comments and insights.

Several other individuals made valuable contributions to this book: Susan Taira, who assisted several trainees with their vignettes when we were not available; Vicki Bartosik, for her assistance with the annotated bibliography; our administrative assistant, Rosemary De La Torre, for her time, patience, and attention to detail; Linda Nelson, who consulted and provided enthusiastic feedback to each draft of the book; Suzanne Wilson, who provided astute guidance in conceptualizing the cases; Far West Laboratory's Director of Publications, Sandra Kirkpatrick, for her encouragement and suggestions; and Michael Alderson, for his editorial advice. A special tribute goes to Lee Shulman, who provided the inspiration for creating casebooks with commentaries by teachers and scholars, and was a source of continual support during each phase of the project.

Judith H. Shulman, Far West Laboratory
Joel A. Colbert, Los Angeles Unified School District

INTRODUCTION

In recent years educators and policymakers have expressed concern about the quality of schools. This concern is heightened by recent studies that show large numbers of teachers leave the profession after the first few years. Teachers report that poor working conditions in schools make it difficult for novices to gain mastery and a sense of self-efficacy in their work with students. These conditions include the absence of materials and books, isolation from other colleagues, and the lack of on-going assistance in learning to teach from experienced teachers and administrators.

Researchers and practitioners point to the first year as the critical year of teaching for it often determines whether a person will stay in teaching and what type of teacher the person will become. Typically, beginning teachers are left to work things out on their own in a sink-or-swim or trial-and-error fashion. In the first few months, they concentrate on survival skills alone, and are likely to focus on what is necessary to keep the class under control. Concentrating on survival skills may encourage beginning teachers to explore only a narrow range of alternatives, and discourage them from continuing to learn to hold high standards for effective practice (Feiman-Nemser, 1983). Thus it is particularly important for newcomers to be supported by outstanding veteran teachers so they can grow beyond the initial stages of survival and coping.

This casebook, like an album of snapshots, provides candid and often surprising descriptions of the struggles of a particular type of newcomer, a teacher who enters the profession with no previous teacher preparation. The cases describe how a committed group of novice teachers grappled with the problems of transforming the content knowledge they had learned at a university into accessible units of instruction for teenagers in inner-city schools. Most of the teachers had never previously attended an inner-city school, and quickly learned that they could not teach using the ways that they themselves had been taught. They were forced simultaneously to plan new units of instruction, to develop alternative methods of instruction tailored to the students in their classes, and to establish a classroom environment conducive to learning.

Teaching in Los Angeles inner-city schools, like any other large urban district, is challenging for most teachers, but particularly for newcomers. Placements are sometimes made mid-year, textbooks and materials are limited and sometimes inappropriate, time for planning is minimal, and students are often unmotivated and disruptive. Moreover, lessons that appear appropriate during the planning stages sometimes fail miserably during their implementation. Nonetheless, the authors of these cases were committed to making a difference in the lives of their students, continued to learn from their own mistakes, and improved their teaching strategies.

The vignettes in this casebook are grouped according to specific kinds of situations and problems that confront all novices during their first year of teaching. All schools and persons within the text are identified by pseudonyms.

The first chapter deals with classroom events — instructional episodes that are problematic either in their conception or their implementation. Three types of classroom events are described:

- a lesson in which the teacher taught a new concept or skill, and the students did not understand it;

- a lesson or unit in which the teacher had no previous substantive background in the subject area; and

- a lesson that included a nontraditional activity, such as small groups or a science laboratory.

The second chapter deals with interactions with individual students or a small group of students who persistently acted out or refused to do work. The cases describe strategies that the newcomers used to diffuse the problems. A common approach was the establishment of a point system for good behavior.

The third chapter examines neophytes' relationships with mentor teachers or other experienced teachers who attempt to provide assistance to the new teachers. Some cases describe how these teachers were helpful. Others recount episodes where the experienced teacher's suggested intervention was not effective.

Each case contains four parts:*

- the academic background and previous experience of the trainee;

- a description of the context, which includes school, classroom, and students;

- a vivid narration of a classroom event or interaction;

- some reflective thoughts about the account.

* See the Appendix for guiding questions to each case.

1

In chapters 1 and 2, each case also includes two or more reactions to the vignette from other educators. These "layers of commentary" as we call them, written by other novices, experienced teachers, teacher educators and educational scholars, add their interpretive comments both to the original cases and, occasionally, to one another's comments. The cases with their commentaries can be studied to infer, extend, or test principles of practice. The annotated bibliography at the end of the casebook serves as an introduction to some of the literature on teacher induction for those who wish to do additional reading.

Authors of the Cases

The nine authors of this volume are practicing teachers enrolled in LAUSD's Teacher Trainee Program, described later in this introduction. Most of them teach in schools considered to be among the most challenging in the district. Eight are currently in their second year of the trainee program. One is struggling during her first few months. Over half of the group is older than the typical teacher who has gone straight through four years of undergraduate school and a fifth year of certification. The teachers bring with them a variety of previous experiences: street artist, waitress and chambermaid; world champion body surfer; 14 years with the San Diego Police Academy; business executive; and three and a half years of teaching English in Colombia, South America. The majority of the teachers also have master's degrees in their designated subject area. Seven teach English or language arts; two teach science. All the teachers share a commitment to making a difference in the lives of their students.

Potential Uses of This Casebook

This book is directed at several audiences:

- *Teacher educators, mentor teachers, and experienced teachers whose role is to educate newcomers to the profession.* Cases can serve as a guide to understanding the challenges and frustrations of the trainees and the interventions that either exacerbate the problems or relieve them. Teacher educators and staff developers can use selected cases as a catalyst for discussing and analyzing the novice experience within a particular context.
- *New teachers.* Cases provide a way of relating the experiences of beginning teachers to those of other people like them so they can overcome the sense of isolation and feeling that

they are alone with their problems. Cases can also serve as precedents to enable newcomers to see how other novices have confronted problems similar to their own so that they can learn from the successes and failures of others.

- *Administrators and policymakers.* Cases provide insight into the needs of beginning teachers from the perspective of the novices themselves. Administrators and policymakers can plan support programs that address these needs.
- *Educational researchers and scholars.* Cases written by teachers provide a strategy of collecting data that incorporate the subtleties and feelings of the persons who experienced the events described.

Though the neophytes in this volume may be atypical because of their lack of formal teacher preparation, the circumstances they encounter are similar to all beginning teachers. The authors write candid, moving accounts of their "reality shock" about events occurring during their first few months of teaching. They frequently describe their students in language that reflects their initial inability to understand youngsters whose backgrounds differ so dramatically. Their descriptions reflect the enormous challenge of encountering two new cultures simultaneously: the culture of teaching and the culture of poverty.

The cases, accompanied by the commentary of other educators, provide an opportunity to learn from another's experience across the boundaries of a school site. They often mirror personal experience, and can be a powerful catalyst for group deliberation about the teaching experience. Group leaders using this casebook as a training tool should be grounded in the knowledge base of teaching — of teacher craft and of relevant research — so they can guide participants beyond "what works" to a commitment to high standards of effective practice.

Case writing can be incorporated into coursework and inservice activities. LAUSD has used this method during a course in staff development for mentor teachers. All of the participants were uniform in their praise for using the technique. They noted that writing the vignettes helped them to reflect on their practices with new teachers and raised their consciousness about the dimensions of the mentor's role. Equally important to the mentors was the opportunity to share experiences and concerns with their colleagues and to learn alternative ways of handling diverse situations. Each case became a precedent for future action. The mentors learned that they were not alone — that their experiences were not unique instances.

Site Description

The Los Angeles Unified School District is a compelling partner for FWL for two reasons. One is the sheer magnitude and diversity of the district. As the second largest school district in the United States, it has over 27,000 teachers and enrolls over 570,000 students. Second, the district's 900 + mentor teachers, funded by the California Mentor Teacher Program, are all assigned to help a group of beginning teachers, in particular teacher trainees.

For the past several years, LAUSD has been forced to hire between two and three thousand new teachers each year. But the district has consistently had difficulty in recruiting fully credentialed teachers. As a result, approximately 50 percent of the newly hired teachers are employed with a temporary emergency credential. These teachers have baccalaureate degrees, have passed the California Basic Educational Skills Test (CBEST), have 15 units in a subject area, and are enrolled in a teacher preparation program at a local university.

The Teacher Trainee Program

The purpose of the Teacher Trainee Program is to provide an alternative route to the teaching profession. Funding for this program was part of the Hughes-Hart Education Reform Bill SB 813, implemented in 1983. Under this provision, school districts may hire secondary teachers who have not finished a teacher credentialing program. These "teacher trainees" teach full-time, attend classes provided by the district, and are supervised by an experienced teacher. Individuals who complete the two-year program are granted a clear teaching credential.

The teacher trainee program provides a means for on-the-job teacher training leading to certification. The program serves less than five percent of the district's new teachers. To enroll in the trainee program, teachers must have passed the National Teachers Exam in addition to all the other requirements for an emergency credential. Once hired, trainees participate in a number of activities during the two-year program: (1) a 15-day introductory set of workshops during the summer before they begin teaching, which includes both "hands-on" visits to local classrooms and small group instruction provided by mentors and inservice leaders; (2) weekly classes taught by experienced teachers in the district; and (3) interactions with an assigned mentor who is responsible for providing ongoing consultation, observation, and coaching. Those who complete the program are recommended for state certification.

CHAPTER ONE
CLASSROOM EVENTS

- *TEACHING NEW CONCEPTS AND SKILLS*
- *TEACHING WITH MINIMAL CONTENT KNOWLEDGE*
- *TEACHING WITH NONTRADITIONAL ACTIVITIES*
- *THE PASSION OF TEACHING*

This chapter focuses on the instructional events in classrooms — those lessons and units that teachers plan and implement with students. What do teachers need to know to plan and implement appropriate lessons and units? (See L. Shulman, 1987, for a more complete description of these concepts.)

- Teachers must know the content of a subject. This is typically acquired at a university during a course of study.

- Teachers need to know about the tools of their trade — the required and alternative curricular materials that are available for any given lesson.

- Teachers must understand how to organize and manage a classroom in general; they should develop a repertoire of particular ways to teach specific topics. The repertoire can be quite rich, including not only conventional alternatives such as lecture and recitation, but also a variety of forms of cooperative learning, Socratic dialogue, discovery learning, project methods, and learning outside the classroom setting. In short, teachers must think through the key ideas of a text and identify several alternative ways of representing them to students.

- Teachers must be able to assess students' understanding of a concept before instruction, during interactive teaching, and after instruction.

- Teachers should understand what diverse students bring with them to learning frequently taught topics, as well as strategies for motivating and relating to youngsters of different cultural and ethnic backgrounds. Equipped with these insights, teachers will be able to tailor their instruction to the needs of their students.

Novice teachers often know a lot about their content areas, but not always the appropriate content for the grade levels they are expected to teach. Moreover, they rarely understand the cultural differences between how they learn a new topic and how their students approach it. Novices do not, however, enter teaching as blank slates in these areas. They come to the classroom with models of teaching gleaned from past experience as learners in classrooms. At the very least, they all have conceptions of how lessons should be taught from previous experiences with their own teachers. Older novices, like several of the trainees who wrote these cases, bring with them additional roles (e.g., parent, school aide, teacher in another culture, business manager) that help them adapt to the teaching context.

When teacher preparation is effective, it gives new teachers the understanding to go beyond mere imitation of their own teachers. In the situations portrayed in these cases, the new teachers have no prior formal teacher training; they are experiencing teacher preparation and teaching simultaneously. Much of their success depends upon the assistance of their mentors to ensure that what results is the education of a teacher, not solely a teacher coping courageously with the complexities of a classroom.

The cases in this chapter describe problematic situations that the neophytes encountered during their first few months of teaching. The accounts depict teachers who are definitely seeking ways to survive their classes. Yet, unlike many novice teachers who merely try to find out "what works" and maintain control in their classrooms as is commonly reported in research literature, these neophytes appear committed to finding educative experiences for their students. Those that have developed productive relationships with their mentors have had an easier time creating such educative experiences.

A new dimension is added in the reactions to two of the cases. Lee Shulman, a teacher educator and scholar, responds both to the original cases and to others' comments on the cases. Shulman also argues persuasively for the value of reflection and experiential learning through the writing of narrative accounts.

Overview of the Chapter

This chapter has four parts. Each addresses a different kind of instructional situation in which all novices find themselves during the first few months of teaching.

Teaching new concepts and skills. In this section, two teachers describe how they tried to explain a new concept or teach a new skill, but failed to help students understand the instruction. In each account, the trainees initially used teaching methods similar to the ways that they had been taught. They quickly discovered, however, that those strategies were ineffective.

The first case, "A Major Overhaul," describes the consequences of teaching a complete unit without providing enough practice during each phase of the unit. In the second case, "Breaking the Barrier," the teacher discovers the importance of providing appropriate motivating activities before teaching a new unit. The last case, "One Struggle After Another," poignantly illustrates the trials of a teacher whose attempts at teaching Shakespeare continue to fail because she misjudges the capabilities, needs, and skills of her students.

Implicit in all three cases is a reluctance by the novices to use the expertise of mentor teachers and other veterans for suggestions on how to plan and carry out units of instruction. The novices sought assistance only when they realized that their students were not responding to their instructional methods. These novices learned that they should seek help before planning new units to avoid unhappy circumstances later on.

Teaching with minimal content knowledge. This section deals with a challenge teachers frequently encounter: being required to teach a subject about which one has little knowledge. For example, an English major can know a lot about literature without knowing much about American Folklore, a unit required in several middle school curricula. How does a teacher prepare to teach such a unit? What resources does he or she use? What happens during the implementation of the unit?

"Saved from Burnout" describes how a teacher coped with such a situation. By December, this middle school novice was exhausted from keeping up with the day-to-day stress of her new assignment, and had little strength to plan a unit on a topic about which she had very little knowledge. She was fortunate to have had a mentor teacher who provided materials, demonstration classes, and ideas for lessons. These tided her over until the Christmas vacation. During the two-week interim she had the time to research various folktales and plan activities for a creative unit.

Teaching with nontraditional activities. One case, "Descent from Innocence," illustrates the difficulty of organizing instruction using nontraditional activities, such as small groups and science laboratories. The case portrays the pandemonium that can ensue when a teacher does not adequately prepare for a small group activity. Like other new teachers in this chapter, this newcomer misjudged the content knowledge and skills of his students, launched a brief review of the topic, and sent his students to solve problems in small groups. What occurred is a teacher's nightmare.

The passion of teaching. The case in this section has been grouped apart because — unlike the other vignettes in this chapter which describe one instructional event — "A Semester of Teaching Reading and Writing" describes a whole series of instructional events put in the context of what perhaps can best be called an unusual instructional situation. This teacher attempts to share how he motivated his students to work hard and be successful after they had previously had to put up with a long line of substitutes. What is demonstrated is how much a mature, dedicated, well-educated teacher with high standards can accomplish with students who are initially suspicious of a new teacher. Also illustrated is the value of a sensitive and effective mentor who can provide continual guidance.

TEACHING NEW CONCEPTS AND SKILLS

A Major Overhaul

Eric A. Steinberg

As the child of almost eternally restless parents, I had little choice but to experience American public education in all its great geographic diversity. We were constantly moving, from San Francisco to Oklahoma to Cincinnati to western Massachusetts, eventually back out west to Fresno, California, then finally — as I reached high school age — to Orange County, California, where my father's psychiatric practice finally began to flourish. Through it all, our family's affluence grew steadily, and the three children (I was the youngest) enjoyed many comforts and privileges, a background which fosters high academic achievement and, in my case, an interest in classical literature. Later, I became involved in the Academic Advancement Program, a campus organization designed to promote the success of minorities and economically disadvantaged students at the university — students with backgrounds radically different from my own.

This last experience led me eventually to the field of education, and now, at age 25, I am a second-year Teacher Trainee at Johnson High School in south central Los Angeles. It is a crowded school with approximately 2,700 students enrolled, 90% black and 10% Latino. Abilities range widely in my English classes; college-bound students are commonly lumped with others who rarely spell their names the same way twice. The so-called "typical" twelfth grader handles junior high school reading materials only passably.

I had entered Johnson in November 1985 fully aware of the students' abilities and limitations, thanks to my experience at UCLA. Unfortunately, the school administrators had not (and still have not) seen fit to provide appropriate textbooks and other materials for my senior expository composition and world literature classes. Instead of remediation, I was expected to provide college-preparatory instruction from essentially college-level textbooks — the only ones provided. I began to theorize why my predecessor had quit without notice the week before.

The students in expository composition presented perhaps the greatest challenge since the course was required for graduation. I opted to postpone the study of grammar and begin with a basic writing model: the five-paragraph essay. Lacking any other resources, I planned the unit — with misgivings — around the textbook. We read how to select and narrow a topic, how to evolve a thesis statement, how to construct an outline, how to prepare a first draft, how to proofread and revise. The

students took a test to confirm their knowledge of these principles. Test scores, although nothing to write home about, indicated that most students had at least been paying attention.

Then came the true test — the essay assignment. Students were directed to choose from a list of topics provided, or to clear another topic with me in advance. Almost immediately I sensed mass consternation, or rather a chilling alienation. Talking about essays had been so comfortable; now they had to write one. I pushed on, offering encouragement and attempting to generate class discussions on a variety of topics suitable for writing. The classroom remained eerily silent. Talking to individual students revealed one serious problem: no one knew how to select a topic! I had expected them to pick up this skill intuitively. Instead, one boy wanted to write about "Why Cory should give me five dollars." I reminded him, and everyone else, that I expected the topic to concern some serious *public* issue. When only about one-third of the students in each class submitted outlines, I knew disaster had struck. Even fewer essays materialized on the due date. Most were rambling, unfocused efforts in one or two poorly written paragraphs. Almost no one had successfully applied even the most basic concepts we had been studying for five entire weeks!

As I mentioned earlier, my students' abilities are limited, but in this case, I suspected that my instructional methods needed a major overhaul. Discussions with my mentor teacher and department chairman, both of whom had been observing my classes once a week, corroborated this interpretation. (Ever since, I have found it a wise practice to investigate my own teaching techniques before pinning the blame for a failed lesson on my students' lack of interest or skill.)

We attempted to identify the mistakes I had made and to rethink the unit by adhering to a couple of common-sense principles which I had earlier overlooked. Our analysis revealed two glaring mistakes.

MISTAKE #1: Beginning instruction with the textbook. The students tend to read abstract material poorly and practically never internalize material presented to them in this way. Few of my students can use composition theory; they need a tangible sense of how a composition should look and sound. What they need, before anything else, is a finished sampled essay — a model to read and to study.

MISTAKE #2: Assigning the entire project at the end of the unit. It makes much better sense to assign the project in multiple stages. Teach students how to select a topic; then have them select a topic. Next, teach them about thesis statements; then have them write one. Next, the outline, with a model provided. Have them assemble an outline. And so forth, until the students have completed the entire project in a series of easily manageable stages. In my first-year teacher's zeal, I had gotten way ahead of myself, attempting to teach the entire essay composition process at once. I had managed to teach absolutely nothing. We had discussed virtually every stage of the composition process from beginning to end before the students had ever been asked to write a word of their own. Naturally, most of them were paralyzed when the time came.

Having identified these two fundamental errors, I felt much more confident introducing this unit to my composition students the following semester. I wrote a sample five-paragraph essay (one typewritten page, single-spaced) as the model to be followed. Rigid, bare-bones structure, no pretentious language, and a topic everybody knew about: television. Every student got a copy of this paper to keep. By referring to this single sheet, I was able, step-by-step, to teach and assign the selection of a topic, the formation of a thesis statement, the construction of an outline, the preparation of a first draft, even the process of proofreading and revision. Even though we had studied these same steps before, almost none of the students had retained any of the information. This time all but a handful of students completed every stage of the project, and while the grammar and mechanics often left much to be desired, the results clearly indicated that most students were comfortable with the five-paragraph essay format. Whereas before no student had seemed to comprehend the requirements for selecting a suitable topic, this time I received submissions on a variety of substantial issues including delicate ones such as abortion and police-community relations — intellectually challenging and socially relevant issues.

Teaching this unit required little or no creativity from me. It did demand that I rediscover and apply some common-sense principles which new teachers are sometimes prone to forget. Especially when teaching students with below-average verbal skills, the instructor must, in my opinion, always remember to use the textbook only as a *supplement* to other, more concrete and accessible instructional materials. These students require a very basic model upon which to base their own efforts. They will immediately become intimidated, and most likely tune out any instruction which fails to begin with a concrete model.

Moreover, the instructor should attempt to break projects down into easily handled, relatively unintimidating stages. Students can then progress through and eventually master, assignments which they would most likely fail to master (or not even attempt) if the project were not broken down.

Reaction

John Shearer (Teacher Trainee)

I really enjoyed reading Mr. Steinberg's account of his disastrous five-paragraph essay lesson and his analysis of the lesson's shortcomings. The new teacher's desire for complete, immediate, and visible results often overwhelms the student's capabilities. A teacher loses effective communication if he spends too much time lecturing to the class or having them read from a book. Additionally, students need to break up large projects into small steps.

I had a similar disastrous experience during my first year of teaching. I spent about two weeks on a unit on the Greek gods. Each student was assigned an oral and written report on an individual Greek god. My students seemed to have a genuine interest in learning about the Greek gods. Because of this interest, I scheduled the oral reports to coincide with my first LAUSD Stull evaluation by the assistant principal. I was shocked; the first six students who were scheduled to give their oral reports were unprepared. The students were embarrassed to tell me they were not ready to give their reports, but I was even more embarrassed to see my brilliant lesson plan flop in front of the assistant principal during my Stull evaluation.

Mr. Steinberg's analysis of his mistakes in teaching the five-paragraph essay are very insightful. The first mistake he points out is in beginning instruction with the textbook. Even if someone were to give me meticulous instructions on how to give my car a brake job, I too would fail unless the person first provided an example. His method of providing a model essay to supplement the textbook is a big help in making the lesson easier to comprehend.

The second mistake, in my opinion, is the larger one. Assigning an entire project at the end of the unit is an open invitation to confusion. Students need to be led through large projects step by step to make sure they do not stray from the path. Given the task of writing an essay, students might become confused while selecting a topic, making an outline, writing a topic sentence, organizing the introductory paragraph, writing the body, or summing up the conclusion.

My current method of teaching the five-paragrph essay takes

five to seven days. It begins with a lesson on locating the topic sentence in paragraphs. Next, I have students choose their own topic for an essay from a list I provide. The third step is to brainstorm ideas about their topic and create an outline from these ideas. I collect their work at this point and give them a grade on their topic choice, brainstorm, and outline. I return this work and have my students create an introductory paragraph. This paragraph is also collected, graded, and returned. If their introductory paragraph is unclear, I write comments on their paper and talk about the problems with them. After this preparation, my students usually hand in good quality work. I give a letter grade for their five-paragraph essay, and then I repeat the entire process once again with a different set of topics. The students who earned high grades on the first essay easily get good grades again. The students with low grades on their first essays usually improve their work and grade.

I think Mr. Steinberg has an excellent approach to teaching the five-paragraph essay. He obviously puts a lot of effort into his work, and he has a compelling desire to communicate his knowledge to his students. When a project does not work out for him, he gives it careful analysis and makes insightful improvements. I imagine that his students are now very successful in their writing endeavors.

Reaction

William A. Rossbach (Teacher Trainee)

Eric's experiences were similar in many ways to those I had during my first semester. I fully agree with his self-assessment and the identification of his two major errors. I disagree, however, with his judgment that his new approach is suited best for "low-ability" students. Eric's amended style of instruction should work for students at any level. It is the amount of work and level of difficulty that should be adjusted to suit various students' ability levels, not the style of instruction. I would suggest also that if this lesson required "little or no creativity" he needs to introduce some. I believe it is a teacher's creativity that determines, as much as anything, the level of interest that can be generated within students. Given a near fifty percent drop-out rate of high school students within this district, a little creativity could go a long way.

Reaction

Karen Desser (Third Year Teacher)*

It sounds like Eric is still in the stage of understanding his students' needs and agendas. Students will find a task such as composing five-paragraph essays hopelessly abstract and worthless unless they are able to see relevancy in it.

It is intriguing that Eric first postponed tackling a grammar unit and instead began with an essay unit. He does not cite a reason for this decision. My hunch is that he felt grammar study would be too "dry" and remote a subject to open with. Ironically, his approach to the essay unit used that same "textbook approach" that he was probably trying to avoid. He realized later that this was the unit's downfall.

The fact that Eric does not attribute any of the weaknesses of his initial approach to the classroom climate hints that class management is not a problem for him. My guess is that he must have a good rapport with his students if he was able to sustain their trust over the five weeks of the unit. Eric can now use that student support to combine with the techniques his mentors have helped him to discover.

Despite the fact that the school seems to lack sufficient materials, it sounds as though collegial resources abound. Eric effectively used the aid of his department chair and his mentor to remediate the situation. He now needs to learn to trust his ability as a young and concerned teacher to tap into the skills and subjects that will be relevant to his students. He seems to have learned from this experience that the method of modeling will illustrate many abstract points. His next step, it would seem, would be to develop student writing to use for class models.

Reaction

Susan Taira (Experienced Teacher)

This teacher's insights and modifications exemplified his willingness to look at his own teaching rather than at what's wrong with the students. The willingness to be responsible seems to be key to changing teaching behavior.

He also made good use of the major support system available to him which includes his mentor and department chair.

By including guided group practice after bite-size chunks of instruction, the teacher was providing a manageable task for the students and feedback to himself on their progress. The model of a five-paragraph essay certainly sounded like an effective teaching technique. Another technique would be the development of a class five-paragraph essay in the same incremental steps as the instruction.

* Except for Ms. Desser, who teaches in the San Mateo Unified School District, San Mateo, California, all the teacher trainees and experienced teachers who contributed to this casebook teach in the Los Angeles Unified School District.

Breaking
the Barrier

Eric A. Steinberg

Teaching literature to students of below-average reading ability poses some thorny challenges. One of my first attempts involved exposing some very unruly twelfth graders to excerpts from Dante's *Inferno*. Naturally, the first task was to motivate them. With a grand total of five weeks' teaching experience, I should have immediately consulted with my mentor teacher for some helpful tips. Instead, I tried my own method.

At home, I worked up a brief one-page overview of the medieval Christian church, radically condensing the textbook's discussion. Students received the final product as a handout. I created an equally brief guide to literary terms and concepts they would need to know in order to appreciate the *Inferno*. To my disappointment, my efforts on the students' behalf went totally unappreciated. Indeed, far from motivating the students, these handouts, minimal as they were, seemed to alienate just about everybody. Only then did I realize how misguided my efforts had been. Intended as helpful guides through the poem, my two modest pages had somehow formed a barrier between the students and the work I wanted them to study.

The problem, I decided, lay in the difference between how I had learned to approach Dante and how these students would have to approach him. Intellectualization, even two meager pages' worth, would not work. The next day I visited my mentor teacher for some other possible methods of arousing the students' interest in Dante. She said, "Ask them to draw hell." Nothing like this had occurred to me, yet immediately I knew her suggestion would work. I also knew that later on, once the students had chosen to invest themselves in the poem, I could gradually inject some historical and literary content into the daily lessons as I saw fit. First, though, the students would simply draw their conceptions of hell.

This assignment elicited an enthusiastic response, and a few truly extraordinary drawings. I posted them on the bulletin boards. Then I drew Dante's model of hell — the nine concentric circles with Satan, frozen in ice of his own making, at the center. I explained that the poem would take us on a journey through the nine circles along with Dante and his guide, Virgil. Then we began reading, without further ado.

Every so often we found it necessary to pause so I could explain a key concept, such as the poem's rhyme scheme, a particular biblical allusion, or Dante's technique of fitting punishments symbolically appropriate to the sin being punished. In fact, the pauses were not too frequent, and I believe they enhanced the students' enjoyment. As soon as I had discarded my own

notions about what the students must know in order to appreciate the poem, they began to respond to it. We referred to some of the drawings they had created, comparing and contrasting their features with the features of Dante's Inferno. We noted how humanity's conception of hell varies from culture to culture, and from historical period to historical period. I challenged the class with a more modern notion they had not heard before: the proposition that hell may exist only as the individual human mind's creation. Finally, as a concluding assignment, I asked the students to draw their conceptions of heaven. (Unfortunately, these drawings, for whatever reason, did not quite measure up in quality or evocative power to the drawings of hell.)

Very often, the success of a literary instructional unit depends upon the prereading activity selected by the teacher. A good prereading activity should appeal to the students on their level. It does not have to be impressively researched or intellectually thorough. Its only objective is to arouse the students' interest. Unless prereading activities observe this principle, the finest efforts will probably come to nothing. In fact, a teacher may only succeed in confusing and alienating the students. On the other hand, just a moderate effort, properly channeled, can lead to an extremely rewarding and enjoyable teaching experience.

Reaction

Anthony C. Gargano (Teacher Trainee)

"Breaking the Barrier" sounded like me. I can appreciate the English teacher's total ecstasy in teaching Dante; however, most, if not all, high school students could care less about it. The interesting thing about this vignette is that the teacher was able to turn a potentially disasterous lesson into one which was instructive, rewarding, thoughtful, and fun. I enjoyed this one very much because of the excitment and depression it created within me as a fellow English teacher. It's a superb lesson in lessons.

Reaction

Joel Littauer (Experienced Teacher)

Eric's road may have been, as he says, thorny, but if he learned the value of motivating students prior to teaching *any* lesson, then the wounds were worth it. And if the pricking of thorns provides stigmata to remind Eric of the lesson he learned, then it was doubly worth it.

The lesson learned is that students are less interested in our vast knowledge as teachers than they are in how we present material to them. Eric's guide to literary terms, while it showed how smart and hard working Eric is, was hardly a vehicle to motivate students to want to study a literary work of the size and scope of the *Inferno*.

The poem, by sheer volume, would be enough to discourage anyone who is not a serious student of literature — and for the most part, our students are not so serious. Before presenting any literature to students, the teacher must ask, "How can I motivate my students to *want* to read this?"

The suggestion of Eric's mentor, to have students draw hell, is a highly motivational approach. This approach, the mixing of media, has a great deal of merit. Music can be used in the teaching of dialogue and of comparison and contrast essay writing. Or, prior to studying *Beowulf*, after an oral reading of Grendel's entrance into Herot Hall and his feasting on a Geat, students may be asked to use their imaginations to describe Grendel, since no physical description of the monster is provided in that passage. The description may be in composition form or a picture may be drawn and colored in.

Brainstorming for items of information on a particular subject, e.g., banking, should precede the reading of a story dealing with that subject. This gives the teacher an understanding of what the students know in relation to a topic which forms the setting of a story, as well as an opportunity to increase students' word banks and cognition levels relevant to that subject. If this is done as a prereading exercise, students will be less apprehensive about approaching the literature, therefore less resistant.

There are many good prereading exercises. Eric would be well served to attend staff development sessions and to learn as many of them as he can.

Reaction

Karen Desser (Third Year Teacher)

I read this vignette after I had responded to Eric's first vignette, "A Major Overhaul." It sounds like his natural instincts are rapidly taking over — this time it only took him a day instead of five weeks to realize that a college instructor approach just won't float.

Eric's analysis of his successful completion of this unit shows his willingness to try new things, and his skill in weaving the hardcore bits of information into discussions when the students ask for or need it. He is again recognizing and accepting that he first needs to tap into the prior knowledge and experience of his students, and then help them to add to, challenge and explore that information. Eric sounds as though he respects his students, and they in turn not only trust him, but actually open themselves up to learning from him as well.

One Struggle after Another

Vickie P. White

As a first-year teacher trainee, I did not know what to expect for the school year. Though I attended public schools in the Los Angeles Unified School District all my life, I realized that students have changed with the times and are no longer the quiet, swat-fearing brood with whom I was educated.

The neighborhood where I grew up, in south central Los Angeles, has not produced many college graduates. My older brother graduated from Jackson State University in 1980 when I finished high school, but no one else in my immediate family had graduated from college when I entered. Therefore, when I was accepted to UCLA, I was proud but not pressured. I finished my English B.A. in 1984, and the course work for my Afro-American Studies M.A. in 1986. While at UCLA, I worked with the campus affirmative action program, the Academic Advancement Program, where my educational pedagogy was largely formed. I was also affiliated with the Black Student Alliance and was active in campus politics.

Before I was assigned to Carter High School, the only other teaching experience I had was in UCLA's Freshman Summer Program. I taught composition to entering college freshmen. I had never worked with the 9th and 10th graders that I work with currently.

Carter's student body numbers approximately 2,700; black students comprise about 90% of the population, while the remaining 10% are Latino. I purposefully sought a position at Carter for I feel that I share similar experiences with the students there and have much to offer in the way of instruction.

Since I began teaching, my English 9B classes have been one struggle after the next. Not only do all of my students have distinct personalities, but they have a variety of skill levels as well. Lessons become extremely problematic when we read. Some of my students are strong readers, but many of them have serious difficulty reading. My weakest readers, however, feel hurt when I do not call on them. Unfortunately, calling on a poor reader often means losing most of my students. Rather than listen to someone struggling to read, many students enter into casual conversation.

When I announced we would be reading *Romeo and Juliet*, the class displayed mixed reactions. Some, mostly girls — true to their set gender roles — showed enthusiasm and rejoiced at the prospect. *Romeo and Juliet*, it seemed, was the most romantic experience they could conceptualize, and for that they welcomed reading it. Other students mostly groaned. "Why?" It was more a plea than a question. "Because . . ." was my response, ". . . because *Romeo and Juliet* is required reading for all 9th graders as stated in the curriculum guide."

Meaningless. They didn't buy it. That was my first mistake in teaching the play. I had not really thought about why I was teaching it. I only knew that I was going to teach it because the guide said so. I did not anticipate that the majority of my students would want to know *why*.

Back in September, I used to incorporate the value of the lesson into my plans, but I stopped because I did not think my students were listening. They also didn't seem to appreciate the reasons I gave for doing certain lessons. Eventually, I even stopped thinking about most of the why's myself. Of course, I had strong convictions about most of the material I covered, but I realized that by not preparing to discuss the lesson's value, I was not ready to have an impromptu discussion. Given the opportunity, I could think of many reasons to read *Romeo and Juliet*, but I was taken by surprise. When put on the spot, I remember beginning to rattle on about Shakespeare, "A new literary form and style for you . . . enjoyable . . . identifying themes . . . *Romeo and Juliet* has, perhaps, one of the most misunderstood lines in all of literature." Needless to say, the students weren't excited.

Before we began the actual reading, I had prepared a lesson to help acquaint students with the language, knowing that they would have difficulty with it. But again, my lesson, my entire plan, was not thorough enough; it just didn't penetrate. Their preconceived notions about the play came mostly from *The Little Rascals* and *The Three Stooges*. I had not anticipated how misguided most of them were about everything in the play. Even the ones who thought it was a swinging romance were in for a disappointment.

After two days of preparation, we were "ready" to read on Wednesday. I assigned parts and we began. I picked my strong readers for the long parts. However, all of the students had difficulty reading. They did not know how to make the language sound conversational. They had not been trained in meter and had no idea of how to stress the appropriate syllable. I stopped often to explain the action and did some reading myself to model tone, pace, and inflections. It was notably tedious and they began looking at the clock very early in the period.

Since Wednesday was official homework night in English, I had planned to have them reread Act I, scene i, at home and write a brief plot summary, just to make sure they were following. They were not ready. My assignment only made the play repulsive to them. I received very few homework assignments on Thursday. This wasn't unusual, but their reactions were. They were grumpy. I think some of them actually tried to do the work, but being frustrated by the language, they gave up. And, during Thursday's class, most of them flipped through the text, counting how many more pages the play was instead of following the reading. "God! Do you see how long this play is. Aw, Ms. White! We can't read this." Some students began to put their heads down.

I realized something needed to be done, but I felt quite at a loss, looking at all of my students' disinterested faces. I decided to try one more thing. I told them I would have some friends over on the weekend, and we would make a cassette of the play so they could hear how it should sound and make better sense of the dialogue. I explained that we would listen to the earlier scenes and, hopefully, become familiarized enough with the language to read the rest ourselves.

On Sunday, I had two friends show up to read a very long play with over 20 parts; I was the only female. One of my friends had had previous drama training at Yale and read quite well. He read most of the major parts, including Romeo. In reading the play aloud, I realized that it was not easy, even for people familiar with Shakespeare's diction. It took a long time, but we did it. I felt like I had taken care of a major obstacle and was ready for Monday.

On Monday, we passed out the texts so that the students could follow the words on the page as it was being read on cassette. When the play began, the students (in all classes) gave me strange looks. One student asked, "Ms. White, are your friends white?" I nodded. Because I am black (and so are 97% of my students), I suppose they expected to hear black people reading. As the tape continued, they would pinch their noses, indicating that one of my friends had a nasal voice. They were listening at least, but barely. Toward the end of scene i, when Romeo enters, they discovered that the nasal voice was Romeo. "Oh, naw. Uh-uh. We can't listen to *him* do Romeo." I was angry because they did not appreciate the fact my friends and I had given up a Sunday afternoon to make that tape. Even though I stopped the tape periodically to ask questions, I still lost most of them. It was time to seek help.

I went to the mentor teacher in the English department who, coincidentally, teaches the Shakespeare elective. I told her where we were as a class and the difficulties I had been experiencing on the unit. She suggested that I not play the tape for them anymore. I had seen myself how they do not listen. She also assured me that if we only read four lines at a time it would be okay, as long as the students were following along and trying. Poor readers were not going to get better by listening to someone else. Eventually, they would get it. In talking to

her, I realized even more so that I needed to be strong in my own convictions before attempting to teach something to my students. Her students know that she loves teaching Shakespeare and she has no problems telling them why. My students, on the other hand, could sense that my attitude about *teaching* the play was lukewarm and, as I'd inadvertently confessed, I was only teaching the play because I was supposed to.

I also sought advice from my English department chair, who suggested that I be more careful in my preliminary exercises. He shared some lessons with me that he uses to help students deal with the language. The exercises modeled tone and influx for the students. I realized, upon seeing them, that they would have helped. He also suggested that I not give reading homework early on. His experience was that students get frustrated, exactly as I had witnessed, and give up. Instead, he proposed that I give my students a few questions related to plot development to find the answers to. As they search for the answers, they would become familiar with the language indirectly. But I couldn't stop thinking that I had "lost" this bunch. Nothing I could do was going to create new interest in the play.

In talking to others and thinking about my failures in teaching this unit, I realize that I was not sensitive enough to my students' needs and capabilities. I expected them to take on heavy reading loads before I had adequately prepared them. I have also read quite a bit of Shakespeare; I have extensive knowledge of his life and works. Yet, I could not pass on or share this information with my students because I did not think out the proper ways to reach them. I based my lesson planning on ideal situations where the students would understand and accept the material the first time I presented it. I did not plan for remediation. Because of these things, it did not matter how much I knew about Shakespeare; I could not convey it anyway.

I am still teaching the unit, and I have used many of the strategies offered by my colleagues. The suggestion from my department chair about not assigning heavy reading homework was very helpful. Not only do more students do the homework, but they have a greater understanding of the material. I also spend more time on lesson planning and am more sensitive to my students' needs and capabilities. It took outside help and suggestions, which I reluctantly sought, to provide me with more useful strategies than I was using. I still feel that I ruined the atmosphere for the play, early on, and that my students will never by very enthused about finishing it. The next time we begin a difficult unit, though, I will not hesitate to seek help initially, during the early planning stages, to avoid unhappy circumstances later on.

Reaction

Joel Littauer (Experienced Teacher)

One common misconception in working with literature resides in the idea that one is "teaching literature," that one is "teaching" a poem or short story, or *Romeo and Juliet*. Vickie's situation is a typical one resulting from that misconception. English teachers teach concepts and skills. The literature, then, becomes the vehicle through which those concepts and skills are conveyed to students. The skill is what is valuable to students, not the play, and it is much simpler to convince a student of the value of learning a skill than it is to convince students of the need to learn a play.

Romeo and Juliet is a play about young love. It is a play about naive children who die because they do not understand the destructive power of hate. It is a play which demonstrates the role luck plays in human destiny. None of these concepts is new to literature. They are good themes before Shakespeare's time, and they have continued to provide good thematic material to modern writers. These themes may be found even in such light fare as a *The Three Stooges* comedy. If Vickie can find parallel themes in a *The Three Stooges* comedy and a tragedy by Shakespeare, then the comedy should be used as an introduction to the tragedy. Given a recognizable vehicle into the play under study, students will find Shakespeare less alien, less fearsome, and the analogy will aid students in understanding what is meant by *theme*, if theme is what Vickie is stressing. The same principle holds true when working within any genre of literature. The teacher must ask, "What am I teaching?" and the answer is never the name of the play, poem, novel, or short story, the text of which will form the bulk of the lesson. The teacher is teaching a composition skill, a principle of literary criticism, or recognition of a piece of the human condition. The literature is simply the vehicle into that instruction.

Drama is not written to be read; it is written to be seen performed on a stage by actors. Vickie's class might be better served by being shown a videotape of a Shakespearean drama after an appropriate introduction. There is a videotape called *The Fonz Meets Shakespeare* which students find informative and entertaining. This may be followed by a class reading of selected sections of Act I, a synopsis, and then a viewing of that act.

The viewing of each act is followed by a lesson in a principle of composition. Students are then asked to write a reaction to the act using the composition skill taught. Writing assignments should be made relevant to students' lives in some way, e.g., boyfriend/girlfriend, forbidden love, luck, just as these concepts relate to the tragedy of Romeo and Juliet. Sample question: "If your parents were to forbid you to date the person you loved, how would you react?" or, "Do you think Romeo and Juliet are doing the right thing by sneaking around behind their parents' backs? Would you?" Given the appropriate writing skill and a relevant topic about which to write, students will be more willing and able to perform as Vickie expects them to. Such an assignment also reinforces students' appreciation of the drama.

Reaction

Karen Desser (Third Year Teacher)

Vickie is earnestly trying to reinvent the wheel, at a school where experienced wheelwrights are just down the hall. In her vignette, she accurately recounts and acknowledges the mistakes she later attacks.

As a beginning teacher at a school with seasoned and gifted veterans, I did considerable foraging before I ever began my units. Vickie could either approach teachers for their two or three most successful strategies for that unit, or could suggest to her department chairman that each teacher share a gem at every department meeting. Armed with those ideas, she would find it much easier to kick off units on a more motivating note. Whenever approaching literature-based units, teachers should strive to incorporate as many game-playing, project-making, creative-writing, role-playing activities as possible. Not only will these approaches engage students more readily, but they alleviate the teacher of the burden of constant paper grading and lesson preparing. I smiled when Vickie recounted spending her Sunday with her friends recording their reading of the play. After two years full-time in the classroom, I treasure every weekend moment as a chance to rejuvenate without having to think about "What will I do on Monday?"

Another interesting spin-off from this experience was Vickie's comment that her students made fun of her white friend's reading on the tape. This would have been the perfect moment to tell the students, "Okay, then let's make our own recording/production of Act I for another class/your parents." Getting students to work with the language instead of struggling against it is always a smoother path into a text. Vickie needs to continue to solicit the help of more experienced guides.

Reaction

Lee S. Shulman, Stanford University

Vickie is a ruthless challenger of myths. A dangerous myth that pervades teacher education is the myth of survival. The myth describes how the newborn infant called Teacher emerges from the womb of the university with only one instinct: Survival through classroom management. As the myth unfolds, the infant copes by managing turns, defining and employing classroom rules and deftly employing with-it-ness, smoothness of transitions and well-placed desists to prevent the otherwise volcanic classroom from its periodic eruptions. Only when our heroic infant emerges from the year-long (or longer) trials-by-misbehavior and can assert that survival has been achieved, is attention then directed at issues of traditional instruction. Only when novices can manage classrooms will they be willing to risk managing ideas.

Vickie challenges that myth with her case report. From the very first day of her teaching experience she begins to think hard about *what* to teach, *why* she is teaching it, and *how* she should go about it with students of differing levels of ability and interest. Moreover, her thinking is not around teaching in general, but rather around the teaching of a particular and predictable text, *Romeo and Juliet*. "Why are we reading this?" is not only a question asked by her students; it is an issue that underlies her struggles with teaching the play. Having kids read aloud in turn, having them review and prepare the text of a particular scene as homework, preparing a tape-recorded version of the entire play read by others — all these exhibit an underlying conception of the purposes for studying *Remeo and Juliet* on which Vickie has not had time or opporutnity to reflect.

What makes the case so tragic, in its own way, is both its inevitability and avoidability. We know that nearly every teacher of English will have to teach *Romeo and Juliet* or *Julius Caesar* or *Hamlet* or all three during the first few years of teaching. We know that nearly all ninth or tenth grade youngsters will find the prospect of reading those plays distressing, whatever their reading level but especially if they are not skilled readers. Would we send astronauts into space without equipment for coping with weightlessness or airlessness? When we can be certain that a new teacher is going to encounter a particularly difficult problem, how can we send him or her into the classroom unprepared with appropriate materials and orientation? Teaching Shakespeare to youngsters of varying skill and interest levels for different purposes requires knowledge of content-specific pedagogy. Knowing

how to get the kids quiet is important. Knowing how to keep them on-task is indispensable. Knowing that you have to create an anticipatory set is laudable. But once they are quiet and attentive, there had better be a meaningful task, meaningfully presented, for them to address. If you don't understand how to present what is to be learned in a meaningful way, that well-managed classroom is going to break down quickly, as Vickie so painfully discovered.

Another myth that Vickie dispells is that there is a special advantage to sharing background and culture with one's students. There may well be some advantage, but Vickie discovers that it is not magical. Having grown up in a similar milieu, Vickie is confident that she can relate successfully to other poor black youngsters. But teaching is more than relating alone. It is engaging in a relationship around texts and themes, concepts and skills, values and attitudes, writings and aspirations. If Vickie is to have a successful educational relationship with her youngsters, both she and Juliet must relate with integrity.

Vickie came into teaching with no formal teacher preparation. I wish I could be confident that any teacher education experience would have prepared her to deal more effectively with the demands of her students and of Shakespeare. Far too few teacher education programs place sufficient emphasis upon a new teacher's understanding and skill in teaching particular aspects of specific and predictable parts of a curriculum to students of different ability and background. When she turned to her mentor and to her department chair, she quickly learned how valuable the "wisdom of practice" could be. They were filled with wonderful ideas, particularly with regard to coping with student diversity and trying out alternative methods and materials. They had experienced the same frustrations themselves. If only Vickie had been able to tap into their knowledge earlier.

Joel Littauer's commentary was exemplary. As I read his analysis and suggestions, I learned more about teaching than I knew before. I saw how the mind of an experienced and reflective teacher can bring clarity and insight into a difficult situation. I would only add a small observation to his thoughtful comments. Another reason we read Shakespeare and other portions of our shared cultural heritage is that those words and ideas have contributed essential images to our shared vocabulary. We read Shakespeare so that the image of "star-crossed lovers" makes sense to us when we encounter it elsewhere (especially in an age when a president regularly consults an astrologer!). Merely reading a synopsis of *Romeo and Juliet* will not help students understand the nuances of "a rose by any other name would smell as sweet." Yet we don't want to see the teaching of Shakespeare deteriorate to a focus on only the particular passages that ended up in Barlett's Familiar Quotations. Studying Shakespeare is an occasion for the learning of essential concepts and skills; it is also an opportunity to enrich our grasp of the English language and some of its most powerful phrases or metaphors. Achieving a proper balance among these goals and the many others that motivate our teaching of classic texts is what makes teaching such a challenge.

Vickie clearly has learned from the experiences that she reports. As we read her account we feel admiration for a young teacher who has undergone pain and has emerged wiser from her analysis of the situation and of the counsel she has received. But we can neither overlook nor trivialize the conditions that made her learning from experience possible. She sought out help and she received it. There were able and experienced teachers in her setting from whom it was legitimate to seek assistance. They provided her with multiple ideas and she was therefore not limited by just one particular suggestion. Most important, she was provided the opportunity to reflect on her experience through the writing of this case report. Notice I emphasize that she reflected *through* the writing, not that she reflected and then she wrote. I am convinced that case writing is an extraordinarily powerful vehicle to foster reflection and experiential learning among teachers. Without such a catalyst, learning from experience is frequently discussed, but rarely accomplished. If we want teachers to profit from experiences, both successful and unsuccessful, the documentation of their experiences for reflective purposes — through case writing and other forms of personal record keeping such as portfolio development — will be necessary.

I am also inspired by Vickie's sustained high expectations for her youngsters. It is so much easier to reduce our standards for poor or nonmainstream youngsters rather than continue to face the challenge that we as teachers must take on: to educate all students to the highest standards possible. Vickie recognizes that teaching the language, thought, skills and images of Shakespeare to her kids is one of the many keys they will need to open the doors of future success. Whether English or calculus, history or music, Vickie exemplifies our educational obligation to keep our expectations high while we search for alternative approaches, representations and tactics to render school learning meaningful to all children.

TEACHING WITH MINIMAL CONTENT KNOWLEDGE

Saved from Burnout

Linda Dmytriw

These are my credentials: a B.A. in Creative Writing, an M.A. in Teaching English as a Foreign Language, an adult education credential from northern California, an ESL testing certificate, a composition certificate and several years of teaching English in Colombia, South America. Along with these papers I have made my living as a street artist in San Francisco, worked with telephone and microfilm equipment, been a waitress, a chambermaid, and a newspaper saleswoman. I have a collection of intellectual, albeit "underachieving," friends and two small children. I was born and raised in Miami, Florida, but most of my adult life has been spent in Colombia and California. My favorite residence has been a houseboat and my least favorite has been a particularly seedy red light *residencia* in Ecuador.

I have always enjoyed literature — as long as it wasn't destroyed through the process of analysis or crammed down my throat. I have a low tolerance for monotonous tasks (e.g. bubbling in grades for computer report cards). And I *forbid* the use of the word boring in my classes. This is the longest I've held onto a job in the States.

It's grueling…holding the floor, planning lessons, and keeping up with the flow of papers, and forms, and referrals. Thirteen-year-old kids — with them it's pent-up energy and out-to-lunch brains. There was a time when I thought my living and teaching in Colombia would have been valuable preparation for junior high school. But the differences in motivation between corporate executives working for international firms and thirteen-year-old Mexican and Central Americans is great. The school I work at is large, about 2,500 students, and primarily Hispanic. Only the teachers are racially integrated — Anglo, Asian, black, and so on. I taught ESL classes last year but now my teacher trainee credential requires me to teach "regular" English most of the day. I've done okay considering I now play the role of Official Representative of Mainstream American Culture to six captive classes of "squirrely" teenagers. Compared to them, I suppose I am middle of the road.

My respect for formal education didn't truly begin until graduate school. Fortunately, I experienced life before rebirth. Professors are smart. Like worms they enter through your insides and wheedle up to the brain. Your personality and values alter; like them, you learn to become meticulously picky and intellectually self-conscious. You strive for excellence

knowing everyone's definition varies. Right and Wrong are relative, yet they're supported by studies, experiments, and tests. The Ideal Lesson is clean, precise, taught. You write your own scripts: teacher asserts this and students respond that. You begin with a text and adapt. You define your own class.

I wonder if LAUSD schools are unique. [As I see it,] most of the teachers must work with texts which (1) are several years beyond the reading level of their students and (2) have content which only partially satisfies the objectives of the course outline. As teachers we must teach students — many of whom are already resistant to the process of formal education — with an assortment of materials that we ourselves collect or write. For new teachers — or any teacher who teaches a course for the first time — this dual job of teacher/materials developer is very demanding. Work begins at the end of the day. Weekends are spent evaluating and preparing. Appropriate worksheets *must* be created. Family and personal affairs are squeezed in somewhere between curriculum design and freeway jams.

Night after night of staying up late and getting up early is hard. If you've got kids of your own, you're under more stress. You can't blow up in the classroom so too often you do it at home. If only I taught four hours a day and had two paid hours to prepare!

It's easy to burn out. I did fine the first part of the year, but by mid-December I was ready to retire. A few weeks before vacation, I was scheduled to teach American folklore for English 8. Never having been a Yankee Doodle flag waver myself, I found it especially hard to get into Mike Fink just before the traditional jinglebells, snowflakes and Santa.

In fact, it was virtually impossible. When my mentor asked what she could do to help, I asked for folklore material — anything. I needed something to hold onto, something to grasp.

My mentor gave me a list of core vocabulary words and visited two of my classes. She told us the story of "Old Dry Fry." The kids wrote reaction papers, and we read another story rich in dialect, "The Man Who Rode the Bear." For two weeks I was treading water. The vocabulary words were my foundation — basic concepts for both my students and myself to grasp. In the words, we swam round and round, spiraling out. We brushed up on dictionary and word attack skills. We did definitions; we alphabetized. We composed sentences and paragraphs. Unconsciously, the legends and songs of

Christmas were woven into the core vocabulary of folklore. We all looked very busy, and the students took a few tests.

There's one thing about public school teaching — everyone's on overload. Although I felt guilty for not knowing anything about Pecos Bill or Joe Magarac, no one else seemed to care. When I got home that last day before break, I dropped my books and baskets of yule decorations on the living room floor. Old Stormalong never entered my mind. Not until somewhere between Christmas and New Year's did I even feel the twinge of a desire to read. My five-year-old boy had an ear infection and my eight-year-old daughter was "bored." So we went to the neighborhood library to browse. We looked up American folklore legend and myth. Materials were plentiful. Academic treatises and annotated anthologies lined the stacks. My little girl was enchanted by the fanciful pictures. My boy fell asleep on a chair.

At home I read, rewrote text and simplified language. I spent a night researching moron jokes and classified superstitions ten different ways. A field that had been alien to me only a few weeks before was coming alive. The core vocabulary from my mentor reappeared in chapter and unit headings. Soon I was analyzing and classifying huge sections of material with zest. I decorated worksheets with xerox etchings and university art. I also xeroxed particularly attractive poems and songs. Although I didn't have many lessons entirely completed when school began, I did emerge from my readings confident, directed, and knowledgeable in selected categories and themes.

I guess the teacher in the classroom next to mine had a restful holiday too because he coughed up a series of one page write-ups on Paul Bunyan, Pecos Bill, Mike Fink, Old Stormalong, and the big baddies such as Frank and Jesse James, Billie the Kid, Butch Cassidy and the Sundance Kid, John Dillinger, and Bonnie and Clyde. In typical fashion, his material was single spaced, badly reproduced but linguistically sheltered. The content was "full." Shamelessly, I scribbled his name on the pages and had my ESL teaching assistant reproduce them each 45 times. These, along with some puzzles and open-ended topic sentences for paragraphs, were my warm-ups for the next four weeks. Back from vacation, I picked up the core vocabulary again. This time I typed it out neatly, supplied woodcut illustrations, and provided proper definitions with lots of examples and models. From these sheets, I wrote up the unit test my principal required.

The Christmas mural had to come down. I brought in a large pastel print of Wyeth's *The Giant*. The kids loved it and wrote lovely descriptions of children standing on a windy beach gazing in awe at the vision of a tremendous giant descending from clouds. My ESL kids covered one of the empty bulletin boards with navy butcher paper. They cut letters for AMERICAN FOLKLORE out of black and trimmed them with glitter. To get out of Silent Sustained Reading in their homeroom, two students trimmed the mural with red and light blue crepe paper streamers. They wound them into elaborate swirls. The corners were fastened with deep red and blue pom-pom tissue flowers made by a hulking 180-pound detention student who couldn't settle down to hold a pencil or pen.

I made several large banners by tearing up sections of brown butcher paper. The kids weren't happy. "Miss, why do you make them so ugly? Use scissors." I brought in Hallmark cards to show them the torn paper technique was OK. Over vacation, I had dreamed up an elaborate scheme for getting kids to write questions and answers to riddles and rhymes. We never did it. In the end, to save time, students brought in jokes and riddles (homework assignments) and copied them onto banners with felt tip pens. If the writing didn't cover a full banner or if a student made a "bad" mistake, we simply tore off the error and began again. Kids worked hard to have their work displayed on the board.

My mentor had lent me an album of folksongs by Burl Ives. We compared his singing with two other printed versions from texts. We also compared Ives' album to the Kingston Trio's. A rather radical departure from Run DMC. Students wrote their own lyrics for "The Big Rock Candy Mountain," another lesson passed on to me from my mentor. Jacob wrote up a masterful graffiti nickname banner just before he was "opportunity transferred" from the school. Traditional lumberjack and Latino street gang names were linked together so they formed an elaborate border for Christian's treatise on "El Lambido." Defiantly, this legacy still stands in the back of the room.

Next to this first nickname banner was another with lots of nicknames especially created by the students for their counselors. Some of my most difficult students, anxious to let out some of their frustration, wrote their most powerful statements of the semester. Nicknames need not abide by rules of sentence boundaries or punctuation.

Sauvageau's Mexican-American folktales, *Stories That Must Not Die*, provided me with high-interest easy reading for substitute lesson plans. When I returned from a bout with the flu, student summaries greeted me on my return. Vocabulary and English idioms my students had never before used were incorporated in their writing. I was astounded at the amazing writing samples from my usually "low achievers." On the other hand, my "higher achievers" who tended to identify more with United States than Mexican traditions reacted coolly to "La Llorona" and "The Perfume that Kills." These kids, I deemed were ready for "Paul's Wife" by Robert Frost.

Because this is a difficult poem, I centered it onto many sheets of white paper, allowing wide margins and spaces between the lines. In the right margin, students took notes on vocabulary, phrases, and cultural information. I broke the poem into artificial stanzas so we could tackle little bits of the poem at a time. In the left margin, we paraphrased each stanza as we went along. In the end, students had to write a summary of the plot. My mentor called this "spoonfeeding" poetry to the class.

My *piece de resistance* was a rather obscure poem titled "The Lady of the Tomahawk," by Tristram Coffin. Basically, it's a blood and guts story that rhymes. It is essentially the story of Hannah, who, kidnapped by Indians, cleverly scalps all 20 of her captors one night while they're sleeping. The poem has great shock value. Reactions from my students were intense.

While Hannah never made my patchwork bulletin board, I do intend to use this American folklore collage as one measure of the success of our unit. Student interest and involvement were high; the end product was attractive and the board remains stimulating even today. I hung two student notebooks with especially lovely covers beside the banners to decorate the wall. Other gaps were filled with colorful bookcovers received from the librarian. One of the roughest samples of writing I ever got was copied over by its author and then translated into "standard." I labeled this work, "Dialect." In this unit just about everyone had the opportunity to excel at something.

Most exciting to me is that now I have the "scaffolding" to do this same unit again next year. I'd like to do grammatical/vocabulary workups for my next door colleague's splendid summaries. I now have two excellent student notebooks for models and am forever collecting Paul Bunyan poems. My mentor and students keep bringing in more. The materials and support are out there for new teachers. It's just that there aren't enough hours in the day.

Reaction

William A. Rossbach (Teacher Trainee)

This teacher's drive for creativity in her work is what makes her a valuable asset to the district. What she says about the amount of time involved in staying a creative teacher is very true, but that is a universal complaint of teachers, if not a generally accepted facet of the job. At first I thought Linda was complaining. At second reading, I think she was simply describing the requirements of a new position. I had a question about her attitude toward students in general given her descriptors "squirrely" and "out-to-lunch brains." But I think this may be an example of her sense of humor and not necessarily detrimental to her teaching.

Reaction

Karen Desser (Third Year Teacher)

Though she would probably pale at the description, Linda's experiences stand out to me as the normal first-year teacher's angst. She has the enthusiasm and adaptability to juggle 400 discrete events in her life and still forge ahead in her classroom.

Linda's professional intuition is right on the money. Before she began this unfamiliar unit, she cried out for help to the pros around her. Using this material to get her started, she then took her own time to discover roads into the material that she could pioneer for herself. As she states at the vignette's conclusion, the next time that she teaches this unit, she will be able to build on this scaffolding. The result over ensuing years will be an even richer unit and a fresher Linda.

One intriguing aspect of this experience, however, was its timing vis-a-vis the winter vacation. Most teachers plan to end their units before vacation, and to return in January to begin a new one. Linda's straddling of the vacation period could have lent itself to yet another fruitful assignment: to have students create their own folklore around their family's observance of holidays. Given the fact that both teacher and students in this situation are familiar with Latin American customs, it might have broadened into a comparison of North American and Latin American culture. Linda touches on this issue with the mention of her Latino students that prefer to identify with "American" issues.

Linda instinctively views her classroom as one of individuals. She cites the diverse needs of her students and is able to encourage them in tasks that are fitted to their abilities. In this manner, she must also look at her needs as a teacher trainee, mom, and all-around person so that she will stay in the classroom sharing her gifts.

Reaction

Gerald A. Richer (Experienced Teacher)

Linda's vignette was extremely well written and flowed with style and character. I found it both illuminating and enjoyable to read. It is also easy for me to relate with great empathy to her teaching situation. Teaching primarily Hispanic children has been my own experience for the last 25 years. There has not been one day I have not looked forward to interacting with my students.

As a mentor teacher for the last three years, I have seen and assisted many young teachers like Linda who were attempting daily to survive and cope with the same frustrations she discloses in her vignette. An underlining theme throughout her vignette and common among my own mentees is that there is not enough time. I would *like* to support her by saying that, as she becomes more experienced in lesson planning and teaching, she will have more time to develop a normal life after work. Sadly, this is not true. Teaching is not just a regular job or even a profession. As she becomes more efficient and skillful, she will find new and even more creative teaching ideas to enhance her classes. But, instead of having more free time, days will become even shorter. This was poignantly stated by one of my former mentees on the last day of his teaching career. As he gathered up his personal possessions and tried to fill out the last official school forms, he told me he was going to go out into the real world and find a job. His last comment to me as I walked with him toward the main gate of the school was, "Teaching is not a job or even a profession. It's a LIFE." In the three months of his now-aborted internship, he literally worked and thought about teaching 24 hours a day. So who are we kidding? To teach effectively and successfully in our district, we need to be DEDICATED, which means teaching will be the major influence that shapes our lives.

Reaction

Lee S. Shulman, Stanford University

Linda is not a naive innocent. She has several degrees and certificates, some of them in teaching as well as in particular content and skill areas. She is a gifted, entertaining and engaging writer. She has taught English to adults in a South American setting, has worked jobs from street artist to chambermaid, and is parent to a couple of young children. She has taught ESL classes in the US. And her first year of teaching junior high-school English to predominantly Hispanic students nearly burns her to a cinder. She doesn't have appropriate materials and feels she must invent them herself. She doesn't understand the topics she is supposed to teach, for example, American Folklore, and is at a loss for finding the time to learn it. She is saved by a combination of her own energy, persistence and intelligence along with timely assistance from thoughtful mentors, colleagues and students.

Like Vickie, Linda is particularly at a loss for how to teach particular subject matter to particular groups of youngsters. She doesn't comment on specific classroom management problems (though she may have encountered some) but on the frustrations of not knowing her subject matter well enough and not having at her fingertips appropriate methods and materials for teaching the prescribed curriculum. Here again, the tragedy lies in the apparent expectation that, as commentator Karen Desser so deftly phrases it, she is expected to reinvent the wheel when experienced wheelwrights are just next door. We would never expect a new physician to diagnose her patient's ills, to prescribe a medication, and then to have to invent as well as fashion the medicine itself from raw materials! Yet here we find Linda with precisely this kind of challenge arising late in the Fall term.

As both Linda and commentator Gerald Richer observe, the central enemy is TIME or, more accurately, the lack thereof. I am reminded of a student teacher whom we interviewed a few years ago. She had previously been a nurse and was not sure whether she wanted to teach after completing her credential program or whether she would return to nursing. She formulated the choice in a memorable, if poignant, contrast. When she was a nurse, she recalled, the work itself was often distasteful, even disgusting. One dealt with suffering and dying, with pain and distress, with disagreeable smells and substances. When teaching primary school children, in contrast, one is surrounded by laughter and activity, with the always unpredictable questions and answers. But when a nurse's day is done, it is finished. She can return to her home, her family, her personal life and relationships, unencumbered by the expectation that she continue to nurse even while at home being parent, spouse, partner and person. A teacher, however, is never finished. There are always lessons or units to prepare, materials to develop, papers to grade, new topics to study and endless other activities that one could do well to prepare. Every hour devoted to home life is experienced as an hour stolen from teaching or preparing to teach. Time is the constant enemy, relentless and unforgiving.

Linda experiences this tension with her parallel obligations as a parent. We are encountering a fascinating new research literature on the struggles of especially women teachers who must constantly trade off between home and school obligations. Although there are apparently some advantages to being a veteran parent when learning to cope as a novice teacher (J. Shulman, 1986), the shortages of time and energy for playing the dual role cannot be ignored. These conflicts exacerbate the already distressing lack of time for planning, preparation and reflection that is a universal element in the life of every teacher, whether elementary or secondary. For the new teacher and his or her mentor, the absence of time contributes even more difficulty to an already challenging relationship.

Some of the most important things Linda learned can probably only be acquired on the job. She learns a great deal about adapting her instruction and her materials to the individual, cultural and linguistic characteristics of her students. Although she doesn't tell us about it explicitly, her knowledge of Spanish must have been invaluable to her, necessary though not sufficient to ensure her teaching effectiveness. Through her own multicultural experiences (I hypothesize) she has grown sensitive to cultural differences and the ways of using culture and dialect as sources of strength on which to build rather than

as deficits to overcome. We see in many of the other cases in this volume how very difficult this kind of understanding is for new teachers who lack Linda's cultural knowledge. She does not know all that she needs to know in a cultural sense before she begins teaching, but she seems to learn how to adapt to and build upon her students' backgrounds rapidly as she works with them.

Careful analysis of Linda's case makes apparent how many different kinds of understanding and skill are expected of the new teacher. She must know her content and the many skills her content entails. She must know alternative ways of teaching her content to students of varying background and ability. She must possess cultural knowledge to adapt both content and pedagogy for students of different language, ethnicity and culture. She must be capable and eager to establish meaningful relationships with students who may be quite different from herself. She must be energetic, persistent, and unbelievably optimistic. And she must find ways to manufacture time when none seems to exist.

Here again we see the power of case writing for the new teacher. In crafting this case, Linda organizes and codifies what she has learned during the past year from her mentor and from her experiences. She uses her substantial gifts as a writer to re-experience the travails of her teaching as well as to celebrate the triumphs. Writing this case not only documents how one new teacher was saved (and saved herself) from burnout. It leaves a legacy that may make all of us who read it and prepare others for similar experiences just a bit less flammable.

TEACHING WITH NONTRADITIONAL ACTIVITIES

Descent from Innocence

Michael A. Miller

My previous experience with the academic world left me wholly unprepared for the events that I would encounter as a first-year teacher trainee. I grew up in a mostly white, upper middle-class community in upstate New York. That I would attend school, earn good grades, and go on to a four-year college was a given. My parents' dream was fulfilled and I graduated from the State University of New York at Buffalo, earning a degree in biology (*cum laude*, too). I went on to receive an M.S. from the University of Southern California in the field of marine biology and was faced with the same problems as nearly all of my peers — find a reasonable job and start paying off the small fortune Uncle Sam had so generously loaned at 9%.

Subsequent to the investigation of several job possibilities, I accepted a teaching position with the Los Angeles Unified School District. After all, who else would provide a full employee benefit package and give me three months annual vacation to boot? I was assigned to Orange High School, which has an enrollment of over 3000 students — approximately 1500 Hispanics, 1000 blacks, 450 Asians, and about 300 other students from a grab-bag of nationalities.

It wasn't until I had been teaching for a few months that I fully understood the odd smile that appeared on the faces of other teachers when I told them of my class assignment: in addition to two periods of biology, I would be teaching three life science classes. Life science appears to be the dumping ground for non-college-bound, nonacademic, potential dropouts. Now I realize that the smile meant, "Poor, naive, innocent soul — like a lamb to the slaughter and he doesn't even know it." Orange High traditionally has had a very fixed and stable faculty. However, recent retirements left a void to fill. I was part of the first shipment of fresh meat sent to the school to replenish its gradually dwindling coffers.

My descent from innocence was swift and brutal. I was given a temporary roll sheet, assigned a room — actually three different rooms — and with little other preparation was thrust into the world of teaching. Suddenly I was faced with classes populated by unruly students, gang members, and other children with only rudimentary scholastic skills. Convinced that with kindness and patience I could help them all if only the students saw my concern for them (what I now term the "To Sir, With Love Syndrome"), and eager to disseminate my knowledge to the masses, I launched into my lessons.

One of the first units I covered was the metric system. Since I grew up in New York State, where the metric system is taught in elementary school, I assumed that this unit would be a brief review for the students. Little did I suspect that, not only did the students have no knowledge of the metric system, they were also ignorant of measuring using the standard English system.

In order to teach this unit, I planned to conduct a brief lecture on metric prefixes and then have a laboratory excercise in which the students measured various objects and converted from one measurement unit to another. I typed up lab sheets explaining in detail what should be measured and in what units I wanted the measurements. The students were then assigned to lab tables, paired off, and provided with meter sticks. What next ensued can only be described as pandemonium.

My intention had been to visit with each group of students and answer any questions that they might have. I also figured this would provide an excellent opportunity for me to get to know some of the students. Unfortunately, as I have found to occur with alarming frequency, intentions and reality often have nothing whatsoever to do with one another.

The first group I visited with was made up of four Hispanic girls. They were having a grand time chatting (in Spanish) about local current events and had given up the lab as a futile exercise. It just wasn't possible to measure their heights with a meter stick, since they were all taller than the stick. Unable to argue with such logic, I proceeded to the next lab group.

I arrived just in time to witness the finishing touches that Juan was adding to his self-inspired metric project. He had beautifully carved his gang symbol into the meter stick with an eight inch knife he had been carrying. He also asked me if, perchance, I would like to buy some "ludes" (quaaludes) from him. I declined his offer, asked him to put away the knife, complimented him on his artwork, and proceeded to the third group.

At this lab table, two young men were having a dispute over a question on the lab handout which directed them to provide the width of their little finger in both centimeters and millimeters. They couldn't decide whether this measurement should be the long or short dimension of a finger. Lerone was strongly emphasizing his point of view with well-placed punches on David's arm and chest region. I managed to separate them and clarify the meaning of the lab question. As I left them to visit with group number four, I overheard David say to Lerone, "This side of the stick is meters," to which Lerone replied, "No it isn't. That's the inches side." Two or three dull thuds punctuated Lerone's response.

At table four, Miguel, who had just been released from jail the day before, was sharing with his lab partners the economics lesson he learned while incarcerated. I listened in and learned from him that half a paper match, split lengthways, sells for 50 cents among inmates. The going rate for the striker part of a matchbook is five dollars. Those in lower economic brackets can borrow the striker from a fellow inmate for the cost of a cigarette. I asked Miguel how the matches were smuggled into the cells, but, as he was about to reply, a blood-curdling whoop drew my attention away to the final lab station, group six.

"Ninja!" shrieked Roger as he leapt from the lab table, meter stick whirling in front of him. Just as he was about to run through his lab partner with the makeshift samurai sword, I disarmed him and banished him to his seat.

Mercifully, the bell rang. "Well," I sighed hopefully to myself, "Only four more periods to go!"

This was just one of many labs conducted during my first year of teaching that didn't go quite as planned. Although none were as disastrous as the metric lab, each one was as much an experiment for myself as it was for the students. Often, I half wished that I had taken Juan up on his offer and purchased a healthy supply of central nervous system depressants. As they say, even the best laid plans sometimes go awry. No conceivable amount of foresight could be used to predict how these students would manage to circumvent reason and rationality.

Now I am into my second year of teaching. Problems still arise during labs, but with a year's hindsight to aid me, most can be anticipated or eliminated. This year, for example, the metric lab went much better. First, I reviewed how to measure in English units. Then I lectured on metric prefixes, prepared several worksheet activities, and quizzed the students on their knowledge before we began the lab. In fact, it went so well that I was able to add study units on the measurement of weight and liquid volume using metric scales and beakers.

I hope that this brief recount of my experiences last year will provide at least some modicum of insight to anyone predisposed to entering the teaching profession. I offer two words of wisdom that I have learned this past year as a new teacher. One is that, while much can be learned from the past mistakes of others, I believe that, in teaching, experience is the only

true mentor. The second is that no matter what, above all else, *never* plan a lab involving rubber bands and raw eggs.

Reaction

Christine E. Emmel (Teacher Trainee)

I thoroughly enjoyed this account of "Descent From Innocence," a proper name, it seems, for this teaching experience. I can empathize with the new teacher. I, too, have assumed that my students knew more than they, in fact, did. My own education apparently was broader than that of my students, with concepts taught in greater depth and at an earlier age. Therefore, I would have expected that they would know the metric system. I still am surprised, even now at the end of my second year, by high school students who cannot plot points on a graph, cannot spell or punctuate, cannot read aloud, cannot take notes from an oral presentation — all skills I had learned quite early. It is a constant struggle to bring the lessons to a level which will ensure some measure of success for most of my students.

This vignette very amusingly described the sometimes tragic results of too-high teacher expectations. Luckily, such experiences, though stressful, help the teacher learn where students are oriented academically. As in this case, the teacher can adjust future lessons to fit the needs of the students. He can learn to test the water to find out how much the students need to be familiarized with a particular subject before he plunges into what might be a nightmare of a lesson. Most likely, this teacher's experience was only humorous in the telling! It was a heartening story of his growth from "a lamb to the slaughter" to a wiser, more aware teacher.

Reaction

Gerald A. Richer (Experienced Teacher)

As a third-year mentor teacher who has supported many mentees in science, I can relate to Michael's story of trying to teach science for the first time. I have taught for 25 years at a primarily minority school composed of students from a lower economic level than those at Orange High, and with reading levels a galaxy behind.

My first reaction to his vignette is one of skepticism. Did this really happen all in one lab, or was this composite of many disasters put together for another Spielberg horror movie?

Whatever, I'll play the game as if this were an accurate account of an educational event in our enlightened society.

I congratulate Michael, first on his survival of the First Year and second on his numerous successes in the second year of his teaching. Many of his difficulties could have been avoided with the help of an on-site mentor teacher. Some kind of pre-evaluation of his students' ability and skills would have been made before jumping into the metric lab. Also, the procedures he wanted his students to follow should have been modeled for them prior to the lab. I find it very useful to use a *simple*, straightforward lab first — one that demonstrates acceptable lab conduct and behavior, safety, observation skills, data taking with built-in success and fun. Don't worry about content, set a pattern first. This could have been modeled for Michael by a mentor in a similar class situation, followed by debriefing conferences after both the mentor's and Michael's own attempt at the lab. Keep records on what worked well, and what you would change next year. And above all, use this when planning the lab again.

I can't conclude without commenting on the obvious. Both district and school policy prohibit the physical abuse of one student by another in class, and especially the possession of a lethal concealed weapon at school. In no way can this be condoned. At minimum, a report by the teacher to school security should have been made as soon as possible.

THE PASSION OF TEACHING

A Semester of Teaching Reading and Writing: A Teacher Trainee's A+ Lesson

Anthony C. Gargano

The Teacher Trainee Program with the Los Angeles Unified School District attracted me when I first heard about it at a meeting at California State University at Long Beach. I was enrolled in a single-subject credential program there with two classes remaining before I completed the program. I chose to drop the CSULB program in favor of the Teacher Trainee Program. The reasons were numerous but here are a few. First, I was dissatisfied being a mobile-freeway teacher. Second, I wanted to get busy with my life's ambition of actually teaching. Third, I would have a steady job with a guaranteed monthly salary and fringe benefits that I never had before. All these pluses attracted me to the program. Further, the program at LAUSD taught me about the practical aspects of teaching — on-the-job training, the only real training that counts — as opposed to the theoretical jargon I had had in previous education classes.

I am neither green nor aged in the art of teaching. I received my A.B. in English from California State University at Long Beach in 1971. I was unable to find a teaching position at that time, so I took a job in retail management. Several years of big money and one ulcer later I decided, no more of this! I was unhappy. I was not doing what I wanted with my life and I was becoming even more unhappy. I quit my retail job and returned to Orange Coast College where I began taking art classes. Teaching positions in 1978 were still not readily available so I returned to school to pursue my second love, art. After one year in the Interior Space Design program at Orange Coast College, one of my instructors asked me if I would like to teach one class. What a break for me. (I was able to get a community college credential based on my A.B.) Although I was not going to teach English, at least I was going to teach!

Three years later and four part-time positions later, I returned to CSULB to begin my master's degree program in English. By this time I was seasoned: two community colleges (I also taught at Long Beach City College) and two private schools. But the best was yet to come. While at CSULB, I was fortunate enough to get a Teaching Master of Arts Candidate position teaching for two semesters. It was wonderful having an English 100 (freshman composition) class. I finally felt that I was going to deal with mature, responsible, intelligent students.

Through all my years of teaching (eight to date) I usually dealt with students 18 years and older — the older the better, I say.

I felt that teaching senior high school students could not be significantly different. And I was right. A majority of students dislike reading and writing, strike one. A majority of students dislike school, strike two. Wherefore art thou strike three? I decided that if I could enter high school with a new teaching approach — an "interesting style" to the basic skills, let's say — then I would have succeeded in changing some souls for the better.

I have always enjoyed reading and writing in high school and college. Why should this not be of interest to tenth, eleventh, and twelfth grade students also? (I know you're telling yourself times have changed and asking "Where is this teacher coming from?" I came from the "old school," the traditional school, like you did.) I felt that most students were turned-off to English mostly because of the teacher's approach to the subject. Since, like many of us, I have had some bad teachers, I did not want to be classified as boring. I was going into the classroom armed with wonderful teaching techniques, experience, interesting reading material, wisdom, blind faith, prayers, and a courage to defeat the enemies of boredom, disinterest, and failure on the part of the students.

I began teaching six weeks into the fall semester of 1985 at Bradley High School. My school consists primarily of minority students and is located in a middle-class neighborhood. Since I was a late placement, the students had already had *eight* substitutes whose names were written on a sheet of paper pinned to the bulletin board. I was fortunate to have the full support of my mentor teacher, the principal, the vice principal, and several English teachers. The day before I started teaching I was taken into two of the classes to check things out. One of the English teachers guided me along as I listened, looked, prayed, and got a little nervous. Tomorrow, Wednesday, October 24, I would have to face them — alone! The next day I was there.

I was disappointed at first. After telling the students that I was here to stay, they added my name to the prestigious position of ninth on the list of deserters. One day I got so angry at their disbelief and disinterest in my instruction and in me that I pulled that list — quite dramatically — from the board and tore it up into several pieces. (Now I wish I had not done that for the sake of documentation!) This was the end of the beginning for me. Human nature dictates to us that we all need a certain amount of security in our lives (the sub list on the wall made me insecure, too), and the knowledge that "someone is there for us"; students need the same thing — someone who will be there for them *every day*. My removing the obituary sub list settled my students down. Without it, we could begin the job of learning.

With all this sub foolishness ended, I found that the students were more receptive to my instruction. When I first entered the classroom to begin my first day of teaching, I talked about *myself*. Talking about Hemingway, Shakespeare, Dickinson, or anybody else would have been an instant suicide. The second day I talked about my class rules and my standards. The third day I let the students talk about themselves.

The fourth day I returned the mounds of papers the students had turned in since the first week of school — you know I had been busy! I placed on each paper either a check mark (for completed work) or a letter grade if I knew exactly what the assignment was about. I had never seen so much paper shoved into drawers, on chairs, on tables — absolutely everywhere. I made it very clear to the students that all their previous work was not in vain. Credit would be given.

I finally began my instruction on the tenth week of school. Grades were due. What a mess! The math teacher who was subbing the class for a week gave the students "I," "P," or "F." There were absolutely no grades in the roll book for eight weeks. I literally moved mountains of paper and got it together. (The prayers helped, I believe.) I was prepared to give honest, evaluative ten-week grades to the students. When the students realized that *I* gave them their ten week grades, it meant business — seeing was believing. Mr. Gargano was here to stay.

My instruction went smoothly from the tenth to the twentieth week of school. Why? I was prepared. I checked the *Guidelines for Instruction* and selected my objectives for the semester for each course. Then I planned my lessons using the LAUSD course outlines for each course. The students knew I was prepared, organized, and ready to begin teaching. This made a considerable difference in my classroom management and teaching effectiveness. I learned and suggest that it is *structure* which students want, demand, expect, and respect. Nothing short of this will bring success to a beginning teacher in a secondary school.

I now understand that many of my students did not want to work for the "new teacher" because they believed that I was going to leave just as other teachers before me had. This made me concerned about my attendance. What if I should get sick and have to be out of school for a few days? Oh no! I felt that my presence in the classroom every day would be another positive reinforcement to my permanence in room 209. During this first semester I was sick for two days (Friday and Monday). When I returned to school on Tuesday many of the students asked if I was feeling better; some offered advice pertaining to my health, while others said they were glad I was back. As the days passed, as the weeks passed, as the months passed, we all became winners: I got to teach and the students got content material and a lot of structure.

I spoke to my mentor teacher dozens of times about my students' confusion about my staying or leaving. She suggested that I continue to reinforce my permanence whenever the issue arose. She gave me positive reinforcement when I showed her my lesson plans clearly written out. Her advice was to continue on task without allowing the students to play. I kept them busy with meaningful work after my lectures and writing demonstrations. "Always have something planned for them," were my mentor's words. I did. It worked, partially; yet, there was an undercurrent, something I could not quite put my finger on.

The reason why some of my students did not perform became clearer and clearer as the second semester came to a close. I was still an outsider in spite of my previous efforts to assure them that I was a permanent English teacher. This ruined many a good lesson plan and ruined many a good night's sleep. It took one entire semester for me to become totally assimilated and totally accepted. Only when summer was over and the new semester began in September were the students satisfied that I was here to stay.

My acceptance by the students rested on one major factor — trust. It was more than trust that they believed me when I told them I was here to stay. It was a belief that I was there for them. They could depend on me. Students began asking me what classes I was going to teach in the fall so they could plan on taking my class.

School is a very important time in life, and teachers can make all the difference in a young person's life. I profess not to want to save every student — although my fantasy world of teaching says I can — from many of the pervading evils in our society today (television for one). I have become a bit more seasoned in my thinking in my second year of teaching. If just one student walks out of my classroom with something they did not walk into it with, then I have succeeded as a teacher, and the student has also succeeded in learning something about him or herself. Some thank me now. Some may thank me in a year from now. Others will never thank me. I do not look for thanks, but it is nice when a student takes time to say it.

Then I feel I have done some good. I have an inner glow of pride and confidence that I perhaps have done something right for someone. For me, this has recently happened. I know I am doing a good job in spite of all the other problems which cause me to become angry, depressed, indifferent, stressed-out, and burned-out. Teaching is now rewarding and all the other problems dissipate into vapor. This is my life.

And my life as a teacher continues to get better and better. My second semester (spring 1986) was much easier. Most of the students knew me and would spread the word that I was "cool" (understanding), "a homeboy" (assimilated and accepted; an honor at my school for a teacher), and a good teacher who knows his "business" and cares about the students. One of the administrative deans in charge of discipline told me that several students I sent down to the office all made the same comment, "Mr. Gargano loves to teach. All he does is teach, teach, teach up there. Lord have mercy!" Now that is special to me. Even the most difficult students know what is happening in the classroom. It is wrong for a teacher to underestimate the sensitivity of even the toughest high school student. They know. But they may never let you know that they know. They too want, crave, and demand structure in a curiously silent (and sometimes disruptive) way. They appreciate you, too, in their own way.

Soon I was more relaxed about myself, my students, and my instruction. I was a "homeboy" because I realized the special needs of my students. I was a good teacher because I believed in and never devaluated my standards: no work, no grade; too much nonsense meant a trip to the dean's office, a call home, or a good lecture. Through this trust ran a deep sense of fairness which the students understood, appreciated, and respected (many have told me so). These two assets — truth and fairness — turned many students to a new outlook on themselves, their school, and their future. I believe that all students need a sense of self-esteem — a sense of pride which must come from a mature understanding of themselves. The teacher merely attempts to supply this through instruction and being human.

A teacher must always maintain standards and never let them fall because of stress, student apathy, faculty criticism, or lethargy. The days of the overly inflated grades have deflated with me: students know (word has spread) that I am a very hard teacher who demands work, regular attendance, appropriate behavior, and seriousness in the classroom. Nothing short of this will be acceptable. If some students avoid me, some will not. They will want the challenge of discipline and structure that I give them. They know it is a key to their future.

Now that I am in the second year, fourth semester of teaching, everything is a solid "B" and holding. As I tell my students, it is much better to be underrated. I have many students I had before and some new ones too. I know the old ones will quickly shape the newer ones into position. Many of my seniors responded positively to their writing experience in expository and advanced composition last semester. They know that reading and writing are essential to success in college and success in the labor market.

Many of my seniors read books on their own. I think I accomplished this because I approached reading as an interesting way to discover new things about yourself, others, and the world around you. (However, I tell them that there is nothing new in the world; everything is just the same old stuff retold in a different way.) I piqued their interest with tidbits of a story — never, of course, telling the ending. For example,

> There was this young girl named Carrie who came to the big city to live with her sister and brother-in-law. She soon took a job in a factory making a couple of dollars per week. Now this was during the Depression and money and work was scarce. Now the important thing is that Carrie commits one of the greatest sins a girl her age could commit during this time. (At this point I end, and the students respond, "Tell us what happened to her and what she did." I then reply, "Read the book and find out." It works. Honest it does.)

One student in particular borrowed my complete collection of the works of Edgar Allan Poe. More than 70% of my seniors read the required novel *The Sound and the Fury* (tough stuff), and some even read *As I Lay Dying*, the companion piece to the former. I told them that I thought *As I Lay Dying* was one of the funniest books I ever read. "Why?" they asked. I replied, "Read it and find out." This gives some students a challenge they want to meet. I asked a former student to write some comments about her feelings about the class:

> I feel that in Mr. Gargano's class he gave all the students the willingness and capability to read. I understood all of the instructions that were given to me so I strived to meet his directions (or instructions) to better my ability in reading. He made me want to read more, not just to read as an assignment. And to this day my interest in reading has improved a great deal. Why? Mr. Gargano made reading a way to succeed in life. In order to know about life and its future you need to know how to read and understand what you're reading. He also made it interesting to today's lifestyles.

Her letter told me things I know and some things I do not know.

Several students have thanked me for helping them with their reading and writing. Two students recently won writing awards. Both students said "Thank you, Mr. Gargano." Is this not enough? They said that I gave them structure, clarity, and mechanics in their writing. They also told me that they have been reading more and that they felt that this helped them with their writing. They also felt that they were better prepared to meet their academic challenges in college because of their improvements in their reading and writing habits. These students understood my basic premise for a successful writer: writing is thinking. A teacher needs to help students think clearly, logically, and with meaning; anything short of this becomes a disastrous experience for the student as well as the teacher. I would really like to share one student's note to me with you.

> Being in Mr. Gargano's class first semester of 1986-87 has helped me with my writing skills. That semester I learned more about writing than in all my school years. Mr. Gargano has a very "special technique" in teaching. He taught me how to organize, value, and approach writing. Those who wanted to learn did not lose interest because Mr. Gargano kept the class interesting by assigning books to read, and daily journals, vocabulary, and essays to read and study. I feel that Mr. Gargano is an excellent teacher, and I am honored to have had him as a teacher. I feel confident I will be successful in my life because of his inspiration, guidance, and needed criticism of me as a student, person, and future adult.

If anyone asks me how I teach reading and writing I can tell them. It becomes more relevant and clear when a student tells you how you teach and what they have gotten from your instruction. This makes the total instructional process more meaningful than discussing seven-step lesson plans.

I currently have my entire tenth grade honors class reading *Wuthering Heights*. (Of course they hate Heathcliff.) I did not have to force them to read it even though I required it for the course. (They each decided they wanted their own personal copy of the book which they bought for $2.10.) They wanted to find out what happened to Cathy II and Hareton and Linton. They found their answers at the end of the book. I have had students read *The Women Of Brewster Place, Linden Hills, The Color Purple, Native Son, Black Boy, Uncle Tom's Children, The Outsider, The House of Mirth, Great Expectations, The Bluest Eyes, The Great Gatsby, Tender Is the Night, Gulliver's Travels, You Can't Keep A Good Woman Down,*

and the list goes on and on and on. I believe I gave my students something very special — a part of me which is reading and writing. For as many reasons to their education as there are personalities, each student grew intellectually, emotionally, and independently. If some realized that they enjoyed reading; if some realized how hard it is to sometimes think; if some rejected reading altogether (as some did), the positive effect is that they learned something about themselves through me. If nothing else, I was a positive role model for them.

I do not profess to have all the answers to motivation and learning. I, too, am still a student at heart. Perhaps because of this I am aware of the never ending process of learning, discovering, processing, and understanding. I believe that my students need me. Ironically, I need them, too.

Reaction

Karen Desser (Third Year Teacher)

Tony makes me smile both with the good humor that oozes off of his pages and for the gifts that he makes available to his students. Tony himself is thrilled with his progress and is clear about how he achieved his success and where he is going from here.

Though Tony does not specifically state what his procedures are for teaching writing (and those tips would be useful to the teacher who comes to high school teaching with less experience than Tony), we can learn many things from his approach.

Tony is a professional. We see him transmit his knowledge and his care through his no-nonsense instruction. It seems that this is how all of his students come to respect him, and how most come to enjoy him as well. A beginning teacher can see that if students experience how caring you are of their academic development, they will sense that this grows from your concern about them as people. Tony's students speak of him as a caring and gifted professional and a trusted adult, which could also mean a friend. But my sense is that they neglect to use these words since it would imply that they identify with him on the same plateau. Rather, Mr. Gargano is always on another level, that of the true teacher.

It is difficult to infer the methods that Tony uses for teaching writing, but as for his guidance in reading, he is clearer. His Scheherezadean method of piquing reader interest works for him as a way to familiarize students with the novel's plot and theme yet does not spoil the gist of the storyline. Another sound and proven aspect, however, is that Tony has steered students toward books with which they will be able to identify. Of the titles that Tony cites, the majority of them are by black writers (black women writers) and focus within the black community. No wonder his students have such high levels of academic achievement and self-esteem.

Reaction

Joel Littauer (Experienced Teacher)

Mr. Gargano has learned the value of trust in his relationship with his students. Trust is the ingredient students value most in a relationship, whether it be with parents, teachers, or friends. Having been abandoned by eight teachers and shown graphically and inrrefutably that those who profess to be their teachers do not care and will not last, it is no wonder that the students initially refused to accept Mr. Gargano's assertions that he was there for them and there to stay. Mr. Gargano's persistence and perseverance won the day for him. Now he can teach his classes, having overcome the handicap created for him by those who came before him.

Mr. Gargano's approach of getting to know his students personally and letting them get to know him was wise. There is an exercise for this purpose called "public interview" which is to be found in a book called *Values Clarification*. The exercise provides structure for "Getting to Know You" activities. Grading papers and returning them to students also helped to underline the idea that Mr. Gargano was serious about his assignment and about them.

"Nothing succeeds like success" is an old saw. The instability inherent in a parade of substitutes in and out of those students' lives could not but provide them with a sense of failure. When Mr. Gargano entered the scene, he was, in the eyes of his students, another bringer of failure. No wonder they refused to accept him. Who would willingly accept failure? In such a situation, the teacher should provide students with tasks which guarantee success. Students, even those with experiences like the one described by Mr. Gargano, do not become so cynical and jaded that an "A" on a paper loses meaning. Successful experiences can provide the antidote for the feeling of failure experienced by students subjected to such a situation.

In short, simply hanging in, being there, doing the work well, caring, acting like a teacher, one who sees himself or herself as the teacher of that class, who projects a feeling of "I intend to stay," will eventually win over the class. Time, patience, love, and skill will win over the class.

CHAPTER TWO
INTERACTIONS WITH STUDENTS

■ Pitfalls of a Peer Relationship
■ Foul Language
■ Reward Systems

In the last chapter, the cases described some specific problems that occurred while a teacher conducted a lesson. This chapter begins with a different starting point — the teacher's relationship with individual students or small groups of students who persistently misbehave or refuse to do work. These are the kinds of students about whom neophytes have nightmares, because they appear to the novice to usurp classroom control.

The teachers who wrote these cases were unprepared for many of the students who greeted them in their classrooms. Some students were unmotivated, disruptive, and sometimes violent. Others appeared to enjoy using foul language and making frequent outbursts as tactics to unsettle their new teacher. The teachers were shocked and dismayed with this behavior and were uncertain how to handle it. The majority came from different socio-economic backgrounds, and had different expectations about how students acted in school settings. They were unaccustomed to the frequency of theft, vandalism, gang violence, and rates of teen motherhood that appeared to be common occurrences in the daily life of their students. The novices had to adjust their perceptions from the familiarity of their own school experience to that of their students. They also had to adapt instructional episodes so that lessons were motivating and relevant. Trying to accomplish this was often an overwhelming effort.

The experiences described in this chapter, though perhaps exaggerated by some of the urban placements, are common to most beginning teachers. During the first months of teaching, teachers go through a period of trial and error, struggling to find the "right" way to teach, to manage the class, and to assert their independence and autonomy in the classroom. As new teachers, they look for guidance because they lack self-confidence in their teaching abilities. Often they feel satisfied with just being able to get through lessons. They take risks and try new techniques, only to fall back on practiced behavioral patterns when immediate effectiveness is not perceived. At times they feel they are unable to handle the complexity they see in the teacher's role.

Appropriate guidance from experienced colleagues is crucial during this period. Too often novices hear from veterans that the primary goal of teaching is to control the students. As a result, the neophytes concentrate on discipline strategies, not realizing that classroom management improves with well-planned, relevant, and meaningful lessons. Mentors must help newcomers plan and conduct good lessons, while simultaneously assisting with appropriate management strategies. As novices gain confidence in their ability to teach, mentors must challenge the newcomers to consider alternative strategies that may be more educative and tailored to the needs of their students. These collaborative activities provide enriching experiences for both mentors and their newly hired colleagues.

Overview of the Chapter

Six cases are illustrative of the complexities of teaching students who are often unmotivated and hostile to the school setting. All of the accounts are honest, often painful.

The first two cases describe the pitfalls of teachers' attempts to establish a peer relationship with students instead of one of authority. Both teachers wanted to establish a humane and trusting milieu in their classrooms but were uncertain how to curb certain students' disruptive behavior. In "The Breaking Point," the teacher illustrates her harrowing experience of crying in front of her students and analyzes the outcome of that experience.

The next two cases deal with teachers' initial shock at hearing foul language during one of their lessons. Though this language may be considered street talk in the inner-city vernacular, the teachers were unaccustomed to hearing it in school classrooms. The cases describe how the teachers handled the vocal outbursts, how they eventually dealt with such language (one year later), and how they modified their instruction to prevent similar intrusions.

Due to some people's sensitivity to seeing foul language in print, some of the words and phrases that could be considered offensive have been deleted. Teacher educators and staff developers, however, may want to substitute more explicit language in their university courses or inservice workshops for prospective or new teachers. Neophytes should be prepared to deal with all kinds of offensive language before entering their classrooms, to avoid situations similar to those described in these vignettes.

The last two cases describe why and how the teachers instituted competitive games or a reward system to ease the management problems in their classrooms. In each case the new strategies appear to have solved several problems. At the very least, the reward system bought time for the teachers to establish their credibility with their students. Some cautions about the ramifications of a reward system are discussed in some of the commentaries that follow the cases.

Like the cases in the previous chapter, these are all accompanied by reactions of other teachers. The last three cases include commentary by teacher educators and scholars. Jere Brophy, a leading research authority on classroom management, connects his comments on the intern teacher-authored cases to the research literature on classroom control and discipline. A bibliography of resources appears at the end of each of the three commentaries.

PITFALLS OF A PEER RELATIONSHIP

The Breaking Point

Vickie P. White

I have always felt that teacher-student relationships were very important; I still do, of course, but now I think of them differently from the way I did when I first began teaching. In September of 1986, with my initial assignment, it was my number one priority to get my students' trust. As a young teacher, I felt the easiest way for me to do this was to establish peer relationships between my students and myself; however, I have never been more wrong in any decision I have since made as a teacher.

It was really not clear why I wanted to establish peer relationships with my students. I only know that it was very important for me to do this. (Perhaps I felt it was a way to remain young, or at least be perceived as the young person that I was. Vanity!) The perfect opportunity came with my fifth period English class. The enrollment was rather unusual. There were only eight students, and six of them were female. I foolishly thought that was my chance to begin a camaraderie with a special group of students. We could get to know each other, and learning would be especially "fun" in this small group situation.

I realize now that my thoughts were extremely selfish. It didn't dawn on me that the students were thinking they were in a remedial class because there were only eight of them. They also thought the class was special in another way.

On the first day of class, the students came in and spread themselves thin in the large, empty room, except for two girls who sat together. I requested that all students move to the front rows so that we would all be closer together. With only eight students, roll call was over in less than a minute. While I was taking roll, however, I noticed that the two girls who sat together initially were establishing themselves as the controlling forces in the room; they were insulting each other as well as the other students, whom they did not even know. "What nerve," I thought.

When I was ready to give my introductory remarks and begin my first day "getting to know you" discussion, it was difficult for me to get the two young ladies to release the floor. I wanted the students to introduce themselves and then work on a paragraph diagnostic I had prepared. "Excuse me," I said. "I would like to start by introducing myself and telling you a little bit about the course." The room was quiet. I thought it was genuine interest, but now I think it was more temporary curiosity. I informed all of the students that they would have

to stand up, speak clearly, and introduce themselves to the class. There were numerous groans, but that had been the case all day.

One of the talkative girls volunteered to go first. I was pleased to see such enthusiasm. She introduced herself as Cynthia Rogers. She was extremely giddy and laughed more than she spoke. I tried to get her to stand still and straight while she addressed the class, but this was futile, or so I thought because I gave up and let her squirm. After she gave her name, I asked her to add something significant about her personality. She made reference to her own sexual activity, quickly getting the sleepy class's attention. I was very embarrassed and found myself only remarking a non-committal "well." What could I say, I thought. I did not want to chastise the girl before I had her trust. "If I do," I thought, "perhaps I will never get it."

Cynthia's friend, Linda Patterson, volunteered to go second. In retrospect, I see that they had already taken some control from me, but it was not clear to me then. Like Cynthia, Linda was giddy with inappropriate remarks. While the rest of the class introduced themselves, both girls constantly interrupted. I did not think it was that bad at the time because there were only nine people in the room. I only made minimal remarks about their disruptions, but never did I point out that they were being rude.

As the discussion continued, neither Cynthia nor Linda waited to be called on to speak; they would cut other students off and blurt out anything that was on their minds. Both of them had some vague notion of raising their hands before speaking, but it was only a notion. Their hands would go in the air and their mouths would simultaneously go as well; it didn't matter who was speaking. I really did nothing to curb their rudeness; after all, it did not seem that bad to me, not then. As long as we were a small group, the class could still function and students could learn.

My small group disappeared the next week. At the end of the second week, I enrolled 19 new students. Unfortunately, Cynthia and Linda were not willing to modify their behavior and accommodate the larger class; they planned to continue talking out of turn and keep the class under *their* control. I also began to sense that it was their plan not to let me accomplish anything in the way of instruction. I pulled both girls aside, still in a buddy fashion, and explained to them that they would have to be more courteous and cooperative in the larger group. They acknowledged that it would be hard for them to change, but they would try. They promised real sweetly, and I believed them. It seemed that they read me as a Sucker (with a capital "S") because if anything, their behavior became worse after that. They hurled more insults about the room, cut more students off, and made jokes while I was presenting lessons to the class.

One day, they were so unbearable that I finally lost my temper and quieted them in front of the entire class. Both Cynthia and Linda had been talking so much that the entire class wanted to see them gagged. I had been writing on the board, and Linda had been harassing all of the young men in the room saying things like "Hey, baby, you should stop by tonight and I'll show you what's up." Cynthia, meanwhile, was picking on one of the other female students, telling her how "ugly" she was. Without giving them warning, I just turned around and lashed out at them: "I have never seen such rudeness in all of my life. I do not understand why both of you continue to harass everyone who comes through this classroom. Linda, a young man cannot pass by without you making some derogatory, sexist remark; and Cynthia, you are always attacking other students for any reason you can think of. Are you both that insecure that you always have to pick on others so that no one will look too closely at you?" They were stunned. The class was quiet. On this day, I think both of them swore that they would get me. Cynthia spoke first, obvious hurt in her voice, "Ms. White, why did you have to say that? You always trying to front somebody off." I thought it was curious, her use of the word "always." Never before had I said anything to either one of them like I just had, and she acted like this was a recurring event. Linda, on the other hand, coolly said, "Oh, honey, people can look at me all they want 'cause I know I look good." The class laughed.

Since then [25 weeks ago] the two have managed to keep my entire class off task for a large period of the time. They are both aware that their offenses are minor and will make me look weak if I have to send them out of the room every day for talking. Cynthia is a good student, with a high skill level. Linda, however, has a poor skill level. I think this inspires her to misbehave. She says, "I ain't gon' do my work because I don't like you, and you're always using them big words," but I know this is largely an excuse for her not to concentrate on bringing herself up to par. I've called the homes of both girls and talked with their parents, but the effects only lasted for three days with Cynthia and were completely ineffectual with Linda. Linda came into the class the next day and said, "Y'all know what? Ms. White tried to call my house last night and

tell on me, but my mama was too drunk to answer the phone." [Laughter.] "See Ms. White what you've done? Now my mama ain't gon' steal me that bike from Sears, like she promised." The class laughed heartily, and I could see that Linda was pleased. She had destroyed her parents' credibility, and now it didn't mean anything to her if I called home.

After that, when I found myself becoming angry with Linda for her disruptions, it was real hatred. I was beginning to feel that I wanted to curse and humiliate her in front of the entire class — and I knew I could. This was all because, I know now, of my failed "peer relationships." My anger was founded on terms that Linda had no way of understanding. She was not used to teachers who behaved as I did. If I wanted to act like a peer, then she figured she was just in treating me like one.

Things have improved a great deal, fortunately. My lesson plans are much tighter so that the class has little room for distractions. Both girls, additionally, practice restraint more than they used to. They also understand that I expect them and the entire class to learn and their disturbances hinder instruction. As the semester progressed, I continued to distance myself from them by behaving (or conforming) to the patterns of veteran teachers, and eventually gained more respect.

It was a really upbeat day, in fact, when Linda came by before class with her boyfriend. "Ms. White, I want you to meet my boyfriend," she said. Then she turned to him and said, "This is my English teacher; she's real smart." She turned back to me and slyly said, "I told him you were cute, too." I was in perpetual shock. For the longest time I thought Linda hated me, as I thought I hated her. She didn't know it, but her small gesture was great therapy for me. I understood that neither she, nor my other students, needed another peer. She needed an instructor, an adult to provide discipline and guidance.

The revelation I had at that moment could have saved me much agony and effort. The girls gave me so much trouble in the beginning primarily because I did not immediately establish a proper atmosphere in my own classroom. First impressions clearly stay with students and it is hard to change learned behaviors. What's more, I realized that even though students test their teachers to initiate them, especially new teachers, their treatment should not determine the teacher's reaction. All students, it seems, want to see how much they can get away with, just how much a particular teacher will tolerate. Once they discover your breaking point, they take you right to the edge every time. I was extremely tolerant, too tolerant, and they took advantage.

When it comes to peer relationships in school, teachers are definitely not students' peers. When I saw that my co-workers had much more control and much less discipline problems all because of their manner, I realized that I needed to change my own manner. I had already modified my behavior somewhat when I first noticed certain attitude differences in all of my students. But, they still have a first impression of me and that still gives me occasional problems. I'm labeled as a "nice" teacher and teachers like me are targets. Now I think I know how to be "nice" but firm so I can't be taken advantage of. Next semester, I am hopeful of an entirely different situation. I have seen many productive changes in the way I relate to my students. When the semester begins, I will know how to handle myself, and them. It does get easier.

Reaction

Susan Taira (Experienced Teacher)

This vignette reveals articulately one of the most common pitfalls for new teachers.

The first question to ask a new teacher is, "What does the *student* need from the teacher in order to acquire the knowledge and skills that would support his achievement?" This is significantly different from what the *teacher* wants in the teacher-student relationship.

The next step is to assist the teacher in the development of rules and consequences as well as the teaching and maintenance of them. When consequences are given consistently and unemotionally, a teacher is less likely to get to the point of losing his or her cool, which usually means attacking rather than directing.

This teacher has discovered what has been consistent with my experience: small groups are harder to control than large groups because of the false comfort that seems to occur. When the group is small, being firm often feels harsher.

It sounds like the students felt the teacher's commitment to them and it was more powerful than the teacher's past behaviors. This explains Linda's act of respect and caring.

Reaction

Donna Colbert (Experienced Teacher)

Ms. White learned some valuable lessons in her first teaching assignment. First, limits (rules) must be stated when you start each new class. You can be as strict as you wish and gradually loosen up as you become more familiar with each student. Second, it would have been helpful if the teacher trainee would have stated her objectives to the class. The students felt uncomfortable and that might have eased their concerns. As for the two girls, they might have been a problem no matter which way the trainee started the class. Some students need special attention. A positive reinforcement technique might have worked. The trainee responded to only negative actions. The concept of calling home is useful if the parents are responsive, but other ideas have to be tried when that fails. It is no fun to go home at night and feel you are hated by your students and you dislike many of them. Of course, there will always be times when you are extremely glad you will never have to see a particular student again. I think that new teachers feel it is important to be friends with their students. Becoming a real "buddy" is misinterpreting the role of a teacher. You are there to provide instruction and guidance. The students have plenty of "buddies" on and off the school campus.

I think that Ms. White learned that you can be a little of both, a friend and a teacher.

Painful Growth

Christine E. Emmel

I moved from a cold and grey Rochester, New York, to the brightness and warmth of Los Angeles three years ago. My immediate goal was to earn a master's degree in biology at the University of Southern California, after completing my undergraduate work at Cornell University. Beyond attaining the master's degree . . . well, that was anyone's guess. It must have been by divine design that I entered the teaching field, for surely I had not planned it. Teaching seemed like a worthwhile option to explore, since I knew I did not enjoy doing research in biology. Also, the job opportunities were abundant — I was almost guaranteed a position if I applied.

And now here I am, a second-year teacher trainee at Maywood High School. I prefer to regard myself as a "first-year veteran," having pulled through the horrendous initiation that Maywood had in store. Maywood High School is nestled between low-cost housing projects and a brewery. The student population is primarily black and Hispanic, the Hispanics now overtaking the blacks in number. Having been reared in the tradition of white, middle-class values and Catholic schools, I was quite surprised by what awaited me — possibly, mortified would be a better word in this case. [As I saw it] gang violence, vandalism, overwhelming rates of teen motherhood, phenomenal records of truancy, student fights in the quad, theft, extreme student hostility in the classroom were just a few of the charms of this particular institution.

During my first year, I was assigned five life science classes, life science being the course of choice for students given the distinction "non-college-bound." I was to quickly arrive at some additional choice appellations of my own to describe these children. However, for better or worse, these were *my* students, *my* wards at least for an hour each day. And I was going to be the best teacher I could be, for myself and for them. Ah, such noble words for the not-so-unintimidated teacher I was in the beginning! "Easier said than done," as the expression goes.

I knew I'd be okay . . . if only I could get Charles out of my fourth period . . . I'd be fine if Jose would come down with mononucleosis for a semester, or if Larhonda contracted an intense case of laryngitis . . . I wouldn't cry half as much in the teacher's bathroom if Steven and Darnell weren't both in first period together! . . . Or maybe my sanity would return if I could just turn in my fifth period to the deck and get a new hand . . . .

Fifth period life science — an incredible group, surely brought together by the grim hand of Fate! The class could see the "new teacher" billboards painted all over me, and they were especially quick to capitalize. Like fresh meat on the block, I'd face a class of hostile, unmotivated, critical fifth-period students each day. Two of the girls, Geri and Ronda, were sisters — an evil alliance. There was Milton, who could never seem to remember to remove his gold earring during school, bring paper to class, or stop talking to Geri. And there was Patrick, who could only sit in the back, doing no work, casting a cold and calculating eye on the proceedings. He would, however, contribute an occasional sarcastic comment. Attendance in fifth period was apparently never a priority to those enrolled, but the few who showed filled the room with their unique personalities.

Not surprisingly, fifth period was to be my point of surrender — surrender to the despair of teaching this hostile and vociferous group, surrender to the frustration of feeling totally powerless over their behavior, surrender to my own feelings of self-doubt and inadequacy.

In the face of my problems with this class, I decided to try "relating" to the students humanistically; this was a suggestion gleaned from several more experienced teachers. My colleagues, including those at my school site and those teachers who instructed us in our teacher training classes, encouraged me to show my "human" side, to tell the class my feelings more as a person than a teacher. It took quite an effort for me to overcome my trepidation at the thought of having an open discussion with my fifth period "horrors." However, I was at the point of willingness to try *anything* that would improve the intensely negative atmosphere pervading the classroom. And so, I would "let it all hang out," or try, at least.

On the chosen day, I told the students that I wanted to talk something over with them, meanwhile easing myself into what I hoped was a non-threatening I'm-your-friend stance. I proceeded to explain, or rather purge, my feelings — how I felt as though they were pitted against me and resistant to what I was trying to teach them, how I felt "real bad" about it and wished we could have a friendlier and more enjoyable class. I finished by "relating" my need for their cooperation, since I wanted to *help* them and couldn't under the current terms of our relationship.

What a feeling inside to finally speak the truth of my feelings — and to them! I looked into their faces, trying to gauge their reaction. Feeling so good about opening up myself, I could only hope for the best. Alas, as usual, reality corrected my forever idealistic expectations, in the form of Geri's comment: "Well, if you weren't such a bad teacher . . . ." This cutting remark, in the face of my vulnerability, plus a few smirks and

and other unsympathetic comments, were enough to push me past my limit.

And so, I *cried* in front of fifth period — something I never dreamed I'd do and certainly one of my more horrible imaginings. I'd never let them know I could be pushed *that* far — and yet, here I was, uncontrollably watering the dirty tile floor! I quickly exited to the hallway, to attempt to regain some equanimity. I hoped no other teachers had decided to keep their doors open that day. After a few moments of agonized I-blew-it thoughts in the empty corridor, I stepped back into my room, heart pounding. In the first second of opening the door, I heard the sound of fake sobs from within. So much for the damned "humanistic" approach! Clearly, neither I nor my students were at a point where this tactic could succeed.

What I learned from this experience is still not altogether clear to me. Once again, however, I was permitted to see that school, just like life, goes on no matter what. I felt I had lost a battle that day and had admitted total defeat in an utterly humiliating way. But a new day of school and fifth period would dawn again . . . and it did. Nothing is irrevocable, and my striving for successful classroom management continued, even though I thought that that one day was The End.

Now, somewhat more seasoned, I can look back and be grateful for the growth I've achieved, growth for which pain is often the price. Motivating my low-level students is an on-going challenge; however, I feel much more confident today, and classroom management is not the big problem it was in those first few shaky months. I believe that students respond to teacher cues, and as I gained experience in handling problem children, asserting controls on classroom behavior, and making the students aware of my expectations, the classes grew to respect me more. No longer am I intimidated by my students, for I see the similarities among the discipline problems in my classes, and I have assembled some basic techniques which are successful with those students who "act out." These techniques include limiting my own interchange with argumentative students, sending out-of-control students to the dean's office with a writing assignment (for me, a page of the dictionary works well!), calling parents, giving students warnings of ensuing disciplinary actions. Students who break the posted classroom rules get their name displayed in the front of the room, with one check for each infringement — three checks in a week result in one disciplinary writing assignment. Of course, I also post the list of classroom stars to balance negative with positive.

I've learned that no matter how bad it can seem, it gets better. In my classroom I have posted some words shared with me by a staff advisor — "Persistence and determination alone are omnipotent — greater than talent, education, or even genius."

Reaction

Michael A. Miller (Teacher Trainee)

Since I, too, am a trainee teaching life science at a black/Hispanic school, I can identify all too well with the situations and emotions described in this essay. Perhaps what this story points out best is the staggering cultural rift between many teachers and their students. This may be especially true of those in the Teacher Trainee Program. Trainees are generally placed in hard-to-staff minority schools. Since trainees often have entered teaching from various professional backgrounds, we are used to dealing with educated and at least semi-reasonable people in most of our undertakings. In my opinion, to be placed in a classroom of uneducated and hostile people is an enormous burden.

This essay points out an important facet of inner-city school teaching that is often ignored. Not only does it take great physical stamina, but more importantly, such work requires extreme mental strength and stability that can only come from within. Many of those who dropped out of the trainee program were people who either did not have strong support systems (i.e., mentors, spouses, friends), or did not have the inner self-confidence that would allow them to return day after day to hostility and beratement in the classroom.

The message that this story relates to me is that before anyone enters the teaching profession, he or she should make a critical personal assessment to identify strengths and weaknesses. Then, a prospective teacher needs to learn how to accept their strengths and weaknesses before students discover and use them to their own advantage.

Reaction

Patricia Norton (Experienced Teacher)

First of all, I needed to calm down from the outrage I felt when learning that Christine, with her background and total lack of experience, was sent to such a difficult situation in the first place! I know of no other business where the employers show such a lack of concern about a person's suitability to a particular job. I was beginning to think that the sink-or-swim attitude in education was phasing out with the advent of the mentor program, but I see, as in Christine's dilemma, that the mentality is still alive and well.

Certainly, in a situation like Christine's, a mentor teacher from that school — one who knows the students and the problems — should have spent time with her initially. The vignette did not mention a mentor teacher, so I am assuming that one was not assigned to her. A mentor could have helped her with seating arrangements to avoid problems. A mentor could have helped her clearly state the rules and expectations of the students with the penalties attached and helped her to recognize when and how to handle offenders. A mentor could have been there with a shoulder to cry on early in the game. A mentor could possibly have put an experienced foot down to insist on the necessity of transferring one of the troublesome sisters out of the class. Christine undoubtedly needed help in gearing the curriculum to the level of her unmotivated charges. It was terribly unfortunate that she came to the point of surrender and helplessness.

As to the advice by Christine's colleagues about solving the fifth-period problem by "showing her human side," I think that the interpretation of what that meant needed more defining. I am one who believes that much of teaching is comparable to show business. In this case, if this approach were to succeed, it should have been scripted, rehearsed, critiqued and tried out on a tough audience before the actual performance. She needed to think out possible reactions and possibly rewrite the scene. As it was, she left herself in a tremendously vulnerable position. Perhaps she could have previously thought out options to offer the students as she discussed what she saw as the problems in the class. An approach that comes from weakness, as hers was interpreted by the students, never works. She needed to come from whatever strength she had left.

I admire Christine's tenacity to hang in there and learn that experience helps. It sounds as if she really has what it takes to be a teacher.

FOUL LANGUAGE

Classroom Trouble

John Shearer

It took me 13 years to receive a bachelor of arts degree in English, graduating magna cum laude at CSU Dominguez Hills. Working outdoors, traveling throughout the Americas (North, Central, and South), and surfing some of the world's best waves contributed to my slow scholastic progress. Highlights along the way included an A.A. in Spanish at Cabrillo College in Aptos, California, a successful house-painting business, and world bodysurfing championship titles in 1981 and 1985. School has always been enjoyable to me, and I have always tried my best to get top grades. Now, as I am about to complete my second year of the Teacher Trainee Program, I try to help my students work to recognize and fulfill their potential.

The first semester of my trial-by-fire, do-or-die introduction to the world of teaching was an agonizing experience. I was hired at Smith Intermediate School to teach English. The Smith student body is composed of a low-income black student majority with a rapidly increasing Hispanic minority. Smith is a school with a bad reputation, but I looked forward to my experience there as a challenge which I could handle. The stories I had heard of violence, theft, vandalism, and classroom disruptions were true, but I never had any fear of physical danger on the campus. My biggest concern was that even though I was an English teacher, I was assigned to teach math, health and science. Additionally, I was not given my own classroom. Instead, I had to travel to five rooms throughout the day.

One of the most difficult situations that confronted me occurred on September 25, my birthday, during my fourth-period, low-level seventh-grade health class. The day was hot and smoggy, with a light Santa Ana offshore air flow. I arrived at school in good spirits, planning calmly and orderly to go about the business of teaching. After my first period conference, I noticed that students in my second and third periods were becoming increasingly restless in proportion to the rising temperature.

My birthday cheer was quickly fading into a birthday nightmare as a rowdy fourth-period health class shoved and shouted its way into the classroom. (Many of the students had failed this class last year, and they appeared as if they really did not care if they failed again.) Most of the students were discipline problems, and phone calls to parents or guardians at home did not change the situation. Typical parental responses included confessing that they had no way to control their children, warnings to the students not to end up like an older brother who went to jail, or making weak, unsubstantiated statements that changes would be made. Some of the worst troublemakers had no home phone, so I could not even make telephone calls.

The lesson that I was presenting in health class that day was on air pollution. I had not prepared a detailed lesson plan because (as most new teachers), I was overworked from other classes. I figured that I already knew a lot about air pollution. Besides, the textbook contained an interesting section on many types of air pollution. My goal for the lesson was to make the class aware of the many sources of air pollution in the Los Angeles area. I planned to ask some general questions about local air pollution and then read from the textbook. I expected the class to be interested in this lesson because of the direct impact air pollution had on their lives.

At the beginning of class, I took roll. A few students were working on the dispatch which asked them to identify at least five sources of air pollution. Most students were talking, and a few were using their modified ballpoint pens to make bothersome whistling sounds whenever I was not looking at them.

I asked for volunteers to name sources of air pollution, expecting to hear answers about automobiles, factories, cigarettes, buses, airplanes, fires, and sewage. Richard, the most notorious troublemaker and leader of the pack, raised his hand and wisecracked, "I know, teacher! Farts!" This response raised a round of boisterous, exaggerated and lengthy laughter and farting sounds from the class, and it gave Richard a feeling of personal satisfaction as a successful comedian.

Richard's response and the reaction of the class took me by surprise, but I knew that class control was very important at this point. I called the class to order and cautioned Richard on his behavior. I could feel the students eagerly awaiting another excuse for an outburst.

They did not have long to wait. Five minutes later, as a student finished reading a page in the health textbook about the effects of air pollution on a person's lungs, Richard began flailing his arms in the air. Before I could call on him, Richard blurted out, "Teacher, teacher! Malcolm just told me to [sexually graphic phrase]!" This must have been the funniest saying any student had heard for months because the howling and whistling did not subside for at least a minute. This sexual slander hit its mark in the minds of 25 teenagers. I raised my voice and in an angry tone I said, "Richard, that is a very rude thing to say!" Then I walked to my desk to get a referral slip.

This was my first opportunity to use the referral slip. During teacher trainee orientation, many instructors had advised us to refrain from overuse of referrals. I had attempted to handle all of my discipline problems through a demerit system, detention, and calls to home, but I needed backup. I sent Richard out of the room and lectured the students on class rules. I stumbled through the rest of the class period, and my composure and bright outlook on the day were shaken.

Unfortunately, I had not yet been assigned a mentor teacher, so I approached the school administration for help. I reported this incident to the seventh-grade counselor, and then spoke to an assistant principal. Both of them understood and supported my actions. This was not the first time they had had problems with Richard. The student was suspended and a parent-teacher conference was scheduled.

The following day, Richard, his old and ailing grandmother, the counselor, the assistant principal, and I gathered in the assistant principal's office. We took turns explaining Richard's overall poor behavior, and I specifically explained Richard's comments from the previous day. The assistant principal was masterful at this conference. She asked Richard if he planned on changing his behavior. Richard gave her a stone-face stare. Then, the assistant principal pointed out Richard's immature behavior and asked him what he thought of himself for making his ailing grandmother come to school with him. Richard was uncomfortable about his grandmother's inconvenience. He was starting to weaken. The assistant principal raised her voice and repeated her question. Richard's eyes began to get glassy. "Answer me!" said the assistant principal. Tears streaked from Richard's eyes. He tried to keep the stone-face stare, but slight convulsions shook his diaphragm. Richard was crying. The assistant principal continued her questions. Finally, the words began spilling out of Richard's mouth. Richard apologized to each of us in the room and agreed to the assistant principal's promise for better behavior. Richard was suspended for two days. When he returned to class he was much more reserved. Although still not a model student, his behavior was tolerable for the remainder of my days with him. Even more important, the behavior of the rest of the class improved.

There were many things that I learned through this unfortunate student discipline incident. I learned that I could handle problem situations. I knew my discipline techniques, with the backing of the school administration, would enable me to exercise ultimate control of the classroom. I learned how to identify the source of trouble and how to deal with it. An immediate and serious response to the source of trouble seemed to be the best solution to this problem situation. I not only removed Richard from the classroom, but this example was also a warning to other students.

I also became aware of the necessity for thorough lesson preparation. With a little more time spent in lesson preparation, I could capture and hold the attention of students. The days that I was least prepared, like my birthday, were the types of days in which students would grow bored and restless. The students, especially the low-level ones, were amazingly perceptive when I was unprepared. At the first sign of dead time, they would become distracted and begin distracting others.

As the next two weeks passed, the behavior of my seventh-grade health class showed signs of improvement. I was able to spend more time teaching and less time on class discipline. This was a big satisfaction to me, and I became more confident in my teaching abilities. I surprised myself with my ability to manage a classroom and teach math, health, and science. There was no doubt in my mind that once I got the English classes I was hired for, I would find success. Fortunately, my math, health, and science teaching assignment ended after four weeks. My classes were dispersed into other rooms because Smith did not reach the level of student enrollment expected. Smith's head counselor gave me a great recommendation, and I was transferred to South Shore High School where I've been teaching English for nearly two years.

I have still had problems with students using foul language in my classroom, but nothing has shocked me as much as Richard's comments at Smith Intermediate. When I hear foul language now, I stop whatever I am doing, look directly at the speaker, and explain that I do not want to hear that sort of language in my classroom. I ask the student if he understands what I mean, and I wait for a response. If I hear the student use offensive language again, I write down exactly what the student says and threaten to call home or send the student to the dean. If the student uses foul language a third time, I write the comment down again and send him to the dean with a detailed account of the classroom comments.

Most students stop using foul language with the first warning. The few that continue get worried when I write down their exact words. Writing down direct quotations is very effective.

After a third offense, the dean at South Shore High School makes sure the student will not use foul language again in my room. The dean threatens to have the student's parents come in to talk to him. This threat usually brings a promise of perfect behavior from the student.

When the student returns to the classroom, his choice of vocabulary words is improved. Other students see this example and they refrain from the use of foul language, too. This helps to maintain a learning environment in my classroom, not an environment of street language. This technique worked during my problems with Richard, and I continue to have success with it today.

Reaction

Linda Dmytriw (Teacher Trainee)

Foul language or the use of street language has been a very real problem for me, too. Because a majority of the students at my school are Hispanic and many of mine have been ESL, the majority of insults, slanders and direct challenges are in Spanish slang. When a teacher doesn't even know that she or another person in her class is even being insulted, she can hardly deal with the problem effectively. All too often the kind of Spanish we run into in the junior high school class is exactly the kind forbidden by university-level language programs. Absurd as this may sound to some administrators who doggedly protect the sterling reputations of their ESL students, I truly believe all new teachers who enter the bilingual environment should be given a slang dictionary. Chapter I, bilingual, or ESL offices should provide them. Insults and inappropriate language which is most often used by students (high-frequency expressions and words) should be spelled out and defined or translated as directly as possible. When multiple meanings exist, we should be provided with them.

Without being able to identify and write down the exact words a student uses, our referrals can look feeble or petty. On the other hand, when obscene language is documented appropriately — dated, timed, and framed inside quotes — we can stay on top of this abusive and potentially volatile behavior. In the past, when a known bad-mouther has rattled off obscenities in my class, I've had a responsible student copy down the verbal garbage word for word. A teacher doesn't always have to understand the literal translation, but it helps.

Administrators, rather than deny this behavior on the part of some students, should deal with this very real problem in a practical way. Teachers *should not* have to rely solely on

bilingual aides to provide translations. A little effort put into truly helpful teacher resources would go a long way. If teachers were less dependent on teaching assistants in this respect, we could strengthen our own control and free teaching assistants for more productive projects and one-on-one student tutoring.

Reaction

Donna Colbert (Experienced Teacher)

I was impressed with the way the situations described in the vignette, "Classroom Trouble," were handled. The trainee used various methods to maintain class control, such as an introductory assignment while taking roll, demerit system, detention, and calls to home. He was not afraid to ask for help. The recognition of the problem and the removal of the one student allowed the trainee to continue with the class. By remaining calm and efficient, I feel that the new teacher showed strength. He did not start yelling or screaming at the students to behave nor did he threaten. The rules were reinforced and the lesson continued. Confidence was shown. The students knew who was the boss and the teacher gained total control of the situation.

First, I definitely admire anyone who can survive an assignment in an inner-city school, especially in a junior high, and still want to continue teaching. There are problems that are unique to this kind of situation. One needs to be aware of the many influences that do not normally arise in schools in more affluent and less violent neighborhoods. Also, there is that wonderful growth process called puberty that seems to emerge during a student's time in junior high.

Second, the teaching assignment was even more difficult because the trainee was not teaching in his content area. This person tried to face the assignment with enthusiasm and confidence which I believe is the key to success in this type or any other kind of teaching situation. The trainee relied on his strong points. When he felt he could not handle a situation, he asked the administration for help. I feel this greatly added to his teaching ability and made the trainee feel successful. Finally, the trainee made a very valuable point, the necessity of thorough lesson planning. You cannot enter a classroom, especially in your first and second years, without complete planning. After a while you know what will work and what will not, but that takes time and continued organization. The trainee realized that the planning phase is important and gained confidence in his abilities to conduct an effective learning experience.

Expletive Somewhat Deleted

William A. Rossbach

My first teaching experience came in September 1985 after four years in the marine corps, fourteen years with the San Diego Police Department, and one year of driving a cross-country semi-trailer. While that might seem less than the most direct route to the classroom, there was about it a general plan. Uneducated upon my release from active military duty, I took the position with the police department largely because the police academy offered fifteen units of credit at San Diego City College. Three years later I had earned an A.S. degree in criminal justice.

When I transferred to San Diego State University in 1979, I changed my major to my first love, English. As inspiring as it was to finally begin work in a field less militaristic, the practical aspect of having to repeat nearly a year and a half of undergraduate work was often a struggle. I left the police department in 1983, and finished the final year at San Diego State as a full-time, non-working student.

When it came time to begin my education courses, I was short of funds and unaware of the emergency credential or teacher trainee programs. My wife and I purchased and operated a diesel truck and leased our services to a major trucking line. The experience took us to forty-six states and so inspired my wife that after six months she got out, in Los Angeles, never to climb in the truck again. This proved serendipitous. It was while she was looking for work in L.A. that she became aware of the programs offered by the Los Angeles Unified School District.

I applied for a position with the LAUSD in January 1985. After participating in the Joint Venture Program, a cooperative effort between California State University and LAUSD designed as a three-week crash course in teaching, I began my first assignment as a pool teacher at Woodward School the following September.

Fully prepared for an assignment in one of the "tough" inner-city schools, I was surprised and pleased when I received a phone call requesting that I appear for an interview at the high school. And when the principal informed me that Woodward was an "opportunity" school, I wondered how I had become so fortunate to have my first assignment with gifted children.

As I was soon to discover, "opportunity" has its own particular meaning within a school's vernacular, no part of which has anything to do with gifted. Woodward School's population is multi-ethnic, roughly one-third black, one-third Hispanic, and one-third Caucasian. They have all been turned off to school, and, in many cases, the school system has turned them off, often transferring them to as many as eight different schools before sending them to Woodward.

I arrived at Woodward at the beginning of the second week of school. Two teachers had already left for reasons unknown. As the third teacher in such a short time, I represented to my students a unique kind of challenge. I was determined, however, that I would be the one to instill in these students the same interest in language that I had. None of the students in my classes had an understanding of English grammar beyond the fourth-grade level, and by the end of my first week I was determined to plunge head first into my quest.

It was a group of ninth- and tenth-grade girls whom I chose to be the first group to whom I would introduce such grammatical terms as person, number, and tense. I knew that adequate preparation for this kind of material and for this particular group would be extremely important. Since all students at opportunity schools work under a contract system, every activity expected of a student must be explained in terms of how many contract points the activity is worth. I thought I had given this due attention at the start of the lecture. I thought I had explained the importance of grasping these concepts so they could put the material into the context of their own lives. I believed that I had created sufficient awareness of the innate curiosity of language so that they would begin to adopt my love of English. My assumptions proved wholly unfounded. The first clue that I had missed the mark came when I had just finished reviewing the notes I had carefully put on the chalkboard. The class had been unusually silent during the first five minutes, and I was excited at the prospect of further explicating one of the salient points I had made when a young lady raised her hand. "What's all this bull, Rossbach?" she said with an endearing smile on her face. "Yeah, where are the f------ handouts for this s--t?" contributed another.

The first two remarks felt like square shots to the jaw, but I maintained composure and attempted to re-explain the entire approach without regard to the profanity. This time the explanation was nearly drowned out by the conversation now in full blossom among the fifteen girls. I stopped in mid-sentence and began to explain just whose class it was and how it would be conducted. I believe that the earnestness in my voice and on my face was having a significant effect when six of the girls walked out en masse. Their parting comments made their opening comments seem like a child's prattle.

I'm not sure what kept me from following them out the door and out the gate, but it was an incredibly strong impulse at

FOUL LANGUAGE

the time. The dean's office provided immediate and strong support. They made it clear to all of the students that I would teach the course in any manner I felt was appropriate, and they strongly emphasized how unacceptable was the practice of walking out. This was not the answer to the problem, but it gave me breathing room until I could make that discovery myself.

The first two periods of the day were my conference periods. I spent these in my mentor's classroom for most of the first semester. I took the time alternately preparing for my own classes and observing his. By the end of the first week of school, he was conducting his classes without any visible indication that he was aware of my presence. It provided me with a theater-like atmosphere to watch what types of behaviors worked with the students and which did not. There were many times when I relieved him for some or all of a class period. This gave me an opportunity to try tactics without fear of losing any ground with my own classes. He spent countless hours providing me with lesson plans and suggestions for better managing my students. These he did on his own time, never letting me know the extra effort it had required. Most of all, he let me see how to interact with hostile students without making it competitive.

He reacted to my recounting of the class's revolt by reassuring me that this sort of incident was to be expected. It wasn't, but he made me feel that way. He served daily as a reliable sounding board. My principal kept abreast of my progress, or lack of it, through conferences with the deans and my mentor. He kept his contacts with me positive and gave strong encouragement wherever possible. Without my knowledge, my mentor was serving as a buffer between me and the school's administration. Because the principal and head counselor were satisfied that my mentor was seeing to my progress, they were in a position to offer nothing but positive reinforcement. I never spent a day wondering what the administration was thinking of me, so I was, in that way, relieved of much of the tension usually heft upon a new employee.

About three months later, I fully recognized why all of what had transpired during that class revolt was my doing and not the fault of either an inadequate system or unwilling students. If I had known the full measure of importance that contract points* had to those students, I would have spent much more time explaining how they would go about receiving them. I could have used the point system to my advantage if I had known how much latitude I actually had in awarding them. Particularly because I was introducing new material, I should

have placed much more emphasis on initial motivation and should have tested the waters before jumping in with both feet.

If I had known how to react, or how to not react, the profanity would not have been as strong a weapon for the students as it was. While I haven't eliminated foul language from my classroom, I have minimized its value to students as a disruptive tool. Its use is too prevalent in the daily lives of my students to expect them to suddenly live without it, and my classes would soon be empty if I were to refer every offender to the dean's office. By calmly, dispassionately correcting students who insist on swearing for emphasis or attention, I have been able to alter their environment in at least one way.

The reaction of that class to the introduction of new material in a new way was more than upsetting to me. It was nothing, however, compared to some of the confrontations I was to encounter over the next three months — including, but not limited to, serious physical confrontations with students. There were many days when the tension and frustrations brought on by the activities in my classroom left me staring at the want ads. I have no doubt that were it not for the support and kindness of my mentor, my principal and head counselor, and the staff in general, I would not be teaching, much less enjoying it, today.

Reaction

Don Kemper (Experienced Teacher)

I would hope that by now this new teacher realizes that even some hardened veteran teachers might have been chased away by these students. The self-discipline and a strong desire to get the job done learned in his previous careers probably made the difference between himself and the two previous teachers.

His maturity and positive self-image are evident in his ability to analyze the appropriateness of his own technique and timing, and to fault them, rather than blaming bad and antisocial children, as the culprits in the problem. I hope that by now he realizes many seasoned veterans do not escape that trap.

I tip my hat to this teacher's mentor for several reasons. First and foremost was the absence, in the new teacher, of any paranoia about the administration and the feeling of being totally supported by all. Secondly, I got no feeling that the teacher felt an immediate need to solve all of the problems. He openly recognized he needed some breathing room to discover what would work for him — a feeling obviously fostered by a wise mentor! Finally, the mentor allowed his own classroom to be used as a laboratory in which the new teacher could observe and experiment in a nonthreatening environment. Here we see the crux of the mentoring process. The mentor communicated a collegial confidence that allowed the mentee to feel at ease while working in his presence. This allowed the mentor to give comfortable constructive criticism necessary for learning and growing. As the new teacher gained confidence about what would work and what would not, the collegial space between the pair diminished.

This is truly a success story about two very capable people. In his final sentence this teacher gives credit to the administration as well as the mentor. Experienced mentors might observe that the mentor was the buffer which allowed the administration to look good.

Reaction

Patricia Norton (Experienced Teacher)

I sincerely hope that William Rossbach didn't have illusions of teaching a classical, textbook style, learning-eager class when he was assigned to Woodward because, of course, he would have had a rude awakening shortly after his arrival. Considering his background and experience, however, his placement at an opportunity school showed some wisdom on the school district's part. At least he was aware of aberrant behavior and had a better chance of survival than most.

In my opinion, all parties in this situation deserve praise. The mentor teacher, in seeing that Mr. Rossbach had the opportunity to observe and test strategies, his help with lessons, and his thoughtful guidance and encouragement through this difficult circumstance epitomizes the worth of the mentor program. My hat is off to this insightful person. The administration reacted in a way that their new teacher didn't feel threatened from above, and was made to feel valued and respected. Mr. Rossbach is to be congratulated for his tenacity and his ability to recognize the help that was available and for taking advantage of it. I hope that his career rewards him with multitudes of satisfying moments!

Reaction

Jere Brophy, Michigan State University

My first reaction to this case example was one of admiration for the level of insight and apparent classroom effectiveness attained by Rossbach in a relatively short time, especially given the fact that he had had only a three-week crash course in teaching as preparation. As he recognizes, part of the reason for his success was the fine support he received from the school administration and the mentor teacher. This kind of support should be provided routinely as part of induction programs for new teachers, although it currently is the exception rather than the rule. I hope that the current educational policy debates and reform efforts produce significant improvements in this regard.

It is worth noting that the mentor teacher provided assistance in planning lessons, not just in managing students. As the pioneering classroom management research of Kounin (1970) originally established, and as many others have rediscovered since, instructional effectiveness and classroom management effectiveness are interdependent. To establish and maintain an effective learning environment in the classroom, teachers need good lessons and assignments, not just skill in obtaining cooperation from their students.

Although he did not realize it at the time, the problems that Rossbach encountered when trying to introduce English grammar at the beginning of the term are typical of those encountered by inexperienced teachers or even by experienced teachers who have not developed the insights that this teacher has developed and thus have not become effective classroom managers. Research has identified a set of dimensions that differentiate teachers who get off to a good start from teachers who get off to a poor start in establishing their classrooms as efficient learning environments (Emmer, Evertson, & Anderson, 1980; Evertson & Emmer, 1982).

At the beginning of the term, the more effective classroom managers take time to articulate clear expectations concerning classroom behavior and daily routines, and if necessary they have their students practice these routines and provide cues or reminders to help them remember what to do or when to do it. They also anticipate their students' concerns and information needs, especially during the first few days of school. In addition to such things as the daily schedule, supplies and equipment, and basic classroom conduct rules, these teachers orient their students to the class by describing their academic goals and planned activities, including expectations and accountability systems governing attention to and participation in lessons, timely completion of assignments, grading, redoing of unsatisfactory work, extra credit possibilities, and catching up on assignments or tests missed during absences. If Rossbach had been enrolled in a teacher education program that addressed these research findings effectively, he might have been able to anticipate his students' needs for information about contract forms and other aspects of the accountability system used in the LAUSD continuation and opportunity schools, and thus might have avoided the unpleasant incident described.

Rossbach's plan to model and share his enthusiasm for language studies was (and still is) a good idea — teacher modeling and communication of enthusiasm and positive expectations are important components of an effective approach to student motivation (see Brophy, 1987, or Good & Brophy, 1987, for a discussion of techniques for motivating students to learn). However, the teacher's inexperience prevented him from implementing this idea effectively, for two reasons.

First, part of the good sensitivity to student needs shown by the good classroom managers studied by Evertson, Emmer, Anderson, and their colleagues was an awareness of the value of starting the class on a positive note. Thus, in the first few days of school, and especially on the first day, these teachers scheduled activities and assignments that they knew their students could handle with relative ease and would find interesting or enjoyable. More demanding and less intrinsically interesting work was phased in as the students adjusted to the class schedule, activities, and work routines.

Second, even when taught by an enthusiastic teacher, grammar lessons are unlikely to generate much enthusiasm for the study of language. The teacher would have been better off to begin with something that the students could appreciate more directly (such as literature appreciation and analysis or written composition), phasing in work on grammar as the students began to appreciate the fact that effective communication embodies good form as well as good content. Teaching grammar is especially appropriate in the context of composition assignments in which the students are writing about matters of interest and importance to them individually.

Although the contract point system in operation in the LAUSD continuation and opportunity schools offers certain benefits (in particular, a clear accountability system that guides student effort in positive ways by specifying short-term goals and the rewards that will be obtained if those goals are met), it also embodies certain weaknesses or dangers that the teacher needs to keep in mind if he is to manipulate it to his advantage. First, this system tends to exaggerate an already existing student tendency to prefer routine and even boring (but familiar and safe) activities over activities that involve ambiguity about exactly what one must do to be successful or risk of low grades due to the difficulty or unfamiliarity of the task (Doyle, 1986).

Especially if points are awarded only for satisfactory completion of worksheets, students may begin to tune out during teacher presentations concerning anything other than worksheet directions and may begin to actively resist the teacher's attempts to conduct discussions or to make assignments that offer more challenge and more opportunities for student initiative and creativity, but also more ambiguity and risk than worksheets do. To minimize these problems, teachers working within a contract point system need to ensure that significant percentages of the total points available are allocated for attention to lessons, participation in discussions, and performance on large-scale projects, not just worksheets and tests.

A second danger inherent in contract point systems, especially if they concentrate on worksheets, is that they tend to exaggerate an already existing student tendency to view completion of a worksheet as an end in itself rather than as a means toward development of important knowledge or skill. Sometimes there is so much emphasis on how many points the assignment is worth and how these points will be allocated that the academic content that provides the rationale for the existence of the assignment in the first place is lost in the shuffle. Teachers need to combat this tendency by underscoring the learning objectives and intended outcomes of assignments when introducing them to the students, teaching the content within a context of application, and including within the assignments themselves elements designed to remind students of the value and application of what they are learning. (For example, concluding worksheets with short-answer essay questions requiring students to summarize in their own words the gist of the learning that the assignment was designed to elaborate or reinforce, state why this learning is important, and tell when and how it would be used.)

If I had been interacting with the teacher at the time he wrote this case, I also would have suggested the following concerning the problem of obscene language in the classroom. Given that the worst of the problem had been solved, a basically effective classroom management system was in place, and he had had time to establish himself not only as an instructor and authority figure but as a concerned individual who cared about the lives of his students, he was in a position to work through his personal relationships with students to attempt to change the attitudes and behavior of the worst offenders through friendly persuasion during private conferences when no other peers were present. I would take two tacks in this regard. First, I would use "I messages" of the type described by Gordon (1974) to communicate to these students about the effects that obscene language has on the class (disruption of activity, transfer of attention from academic content to rule enforcement issues) and on myself as the teacher (frustration, discouragement, anger at what amounts to unjustified mistreatment). Second, I would try to persuade these students that habitual obscenity is contrary to their own best interests. It is not "cool," as it might be if these were nine or ten year olds; on the contrary, it suggests immaturity, inordinate need for attention, lack of social sophistication, and the like. Such behavior is probably costing these students credibility and respect among the peer group even now, and if not corrected, will almost certainly cost them dearly in the future by closing off occupational and social opportunities.

If presented with the appropriate attitude of concern for the students' personal well-being (i.e., not just the teacher's desire for an orderly classroom), socialization messages such as these can help eliminate some of the undesirable motives that drive provocative student behavior and cause the students to adopt more desirable attitudes and beliefs about appropriate behavior (see Brophy, 1985, and Good & Brophy, 1987, for discussion of problem-solving conferences with students and strategies for helping students to develop internalized self-control mechanisms).

References

Brophy, J. (1985). Classroom management as instruction: Socializing self-guidance in students. *Theory Into Practice, 24,* 233-240.

Brophy, J. (1987). Socializing students' motivation to learn. In M. L. Maehr & D. A. Kleiber (Eds.), *Advances in motivation and achievement* (vol. V). Greenwich, CT: JAI Press. (pp. 181-210).

Doyle, W. (1986). Classroom organization and management. In M. C. Wittrock (Ed.), *Handbook of research on teaching* (3rd ed.). New York: Macmillan. (pp. 392-431).

Emmer, E., Evertson, C., & Anderson, L. (1980). Effective classroom management at the beginning of the school year. *Elementary School Journal, 80,* 219-231.

Evertson, C., & Emmer, E. (1982). Effective management at the beginning of the school year in junior high classes. *Journal of Educational Psychology, 74,* 485-498.

Good, T., & Brophy, J. (1987). *Looking in classrooms* (4th ed.). New York: Harper and Row.

Gordon, T. (1974). *T.E.T.: Teacher effectiveness training.* New York: David McKay.

Kounin, J. (1970). *Discipline and group management in classrooms.* New York: Holt, Rinehart, & Winston.

REWARD SYSTEMS

The Points

Eric A. Steinberg

Oh God, not again, you think. Ten minutes earlier you had wrapped up your presentation and launched the students on a writing assignment. Now, with half an hour remaining in third period, virtually no one is working. Five or six clusters of varying sizes have formed, each one generating its own tumultuous cacophony. Two oversized boys begin roughhousing in the corner, their playfulness appearing to edge ever closer to genuine hostility. One or two students, the class "nerd" or the quiet girl in the front, struggle pathetically to concentrate on the assignment. Candy bars and Cheetos are being freely consumed. George, your nemesis, struts clownishly across the room, inducing a violent explosion of laughter and further intensifying the chaos. Perhaps he was trying to impress that same trio of girls. Your head darts this way and that, diverted by violent eruptions everywhere. Now what?

Nearly all inner-city classroom teachers, new and experienced alike, have encountered this kind of situation more times than they would care to remember. Given the radical demands heaped on them not only as instructors but also as disciplinarians, it is perhaps small wonder that teachers have tended to adopt radically different methods for managing their classrooms. As a new teacher constantly seeking advice, I lost little time exposing myself to these various methods. My mentor teacher, for instance, embodied what I would call the "old school" of classroom management philosophy (still the dominant philosophy, by the way). When approaching her about a problem student in my fifth-period American lit. class, for instance, she would advise me to "become a lion tamer: go in there with the chair and whip." In other words,

1. Take a very aggressive disciplinary posture, confronting every offense of class rules — no matter how minor, no matter how frequent.
2. Confront even overtly hostile students directly.
3. Devote a great deal of time to parent contacts.
4. Assume a high level of support from the school administration.

These principles had always worked for her. She was a 64-year-old, tiny, matronly female. I was a 25-year-old, boyish-looking male. What worked for my mentor would not necessarily work for me. In fact, her advice proved almost disastrous. Students greeted my increased strictness with redoubled hostility. For the first time, I felt myself being sucked into overtly hostile confrontations with my students, a few of

which nearly saw fists start flying. Sadly, I was more often than not the one who wanted to throw the first punch! This — despite my clearly posted and universally distributed copies of class rules, my demerit system, my dogged insistence upon throwing away all food and chewing gum, my refusal to tolerate tardiness, unpreparedness, disruptions, minor vandalism, and all the other offenses — I witnessed 800 times a day.

The fact is, I felt silly in the role of a harsh disciplinarian. Of course, I recognized the need for effective discipline in the classroom, but I preferred to weave a more diaphanous web around my students. I felt more comfortable enforcing rules much more gently, in a more low-key, indirect manner. As teachers, we become truly transparent to our students, especially when we administer discipline. Students will exploit every insincere or hesitant word or gesture. I gradually learned this and began to trust my own natural approach as the months passed by. It paid great dividends in reduced stress during the second semester.

My good friend and fellow English teacher began to supplant my mentor as chief methodological influence over me. He and I shared much more in common: we were both relatively young, inexperienced, liberally educated, male, and white. He also had a year's extra experience, for which I became very grateful.

He advised me to loosen up, to play classroom games with my students (every day if necessary), to drop the elaborate grading and disciplinary schemes. "Keep it simple, fun, and entertaining," he would always insist. His classes could be described as noisy but good-natured. Some days he even achieved relative quiet and high interest level all at once! At first I dared not take him seriously. After a few more weeks of severe tension headaches due to high-stress confrontations with students, I began to relent. Following my friend's lead, I instituted some classroom games to be played for half an hour each Friday: Bingo or Card Sharks or whatever, using our study questions for the current week as material for the games. Winning players and teams received tangible rewards, such as candy or free time or even participation points. The demerit system quietly disappeared. The rules did not, for I could sense it had become much easier already to enforce them.

Soon I had divided each class into two teams which competed daily for rewards. Good participation and behavior would earn points every minute of every day — points kept clearly displayed on a scoreboard, a large plastic poster frame with blank white posterboard inside, at the front of class. Offenses against class standards resulted in points for the other team and personal consequences for the offender.

I had stumbled onto a cardinal rule of classroom management: provide immediately tangible rewards and consequences for students' good and bad behavior. My students warmed up to me more than I had ever thought possible, even some of those who had formerly behaved in the most hostile, rude, and incorrigible ways. One student in world literature, a particularly jaded senior who had been barely passing, suddenly turned his entire performance around. He volunteered daily to read aloud. He spearheaded class discussions with keen insights into works such as *Macbeth* and *Candide*, and he began to submit superbly creative and idiosyncratic essays on the course material. When I asked him what inspired this radical change, he did not hesitate to reply: "The points!"

Without a doubt, the new format of games, scores, and points had finally made me more understandable and accessible to the students. This new strategy did, however, have its drawbacks. For one thing, misbehavior by no means disappeared, though it had decreased dramatically in all classes. Some hours would degenerate into ugly and childish feuds, and some students simply did not choose to participate in any way. Surprisingly, almost no one complained that playing games seemed childish. I had expected this to be one major obstacle in getting the new system started. There was also the problem of bookkeeping, i.e., keeping record of every team's score on a daily basis, and of individual winners in other classroom games. Finally, I did invest a few dollars in prizes, mostly at the end of each five-week grading period. Still, these sacrifices proved well worth their cost. I was actually saving great quantities of effort, handling my emotions much more effectively, and, most importantly, teaching a good deal more!

Previously, I had felt bitter about the school administration's failure to support its teachers effectively. Besides my often abrasive contacts with students, I experienced many stressful encounters with vice principals and deans whom I considered ineffective. Parent conferences also seemed to accomplished little. Now I had very little need for the school administration, or for parent contacts. We left one another alone much more often, and everyone enjoyed the new independence. I felt much more in control of my classroom, and more confident in handling any misbehavior that might arise by myself.

This year I drastically streamlined and conventionalized my classroom management, but have also continued to keep it founded on the same gentle, low-key, and good-natured principles. The games continue, although the daily and weekly scoreboards have gone. Good behavior and participation still receive tangible rewards. Misbehavior is now punished with a more mainstream system of check marks, with each additional mark carrying a slightly more serious consequence. In other words, I am steering a much more moderate course this year, somewhere between the radical extremes which I explored as a brand new teacher. I believe it doesn't really matter what specific methods a teacher uses to instruct and discipline his students. The key lies in finding a serious yet credible system that meshes with one's personality.

Reaction

Anthony C. Gargano (Teacher Trainee)

I liked the way in which the writer approached the topic of classroom discipline. A thorough history of himself, his classes, and his technique were quite lucid. The picture of the classroom was more than reminiscent: it had a visual power and relevance to all teachers. The writer's seeking advice from his mentor was priceless, especially when he admits that it was disastrous for him. It was nice to know that he had someone else to "comfort" him. The other male teacher's advice was somewhat realistic. It is through the writing of this paper that this teacher discovered for himself that a system of classroom discipline must blend well with the teacher's individual personality. I believe that this is an enlightening and valuable concept beginning teachers need to read about. The system of points and games became secondary to the writer's point that both good and bad behavior must be confronted at that moment. For the male student who was not doing any work, the point system did motivate him to at least read for the glory of the points; however, this student must also be made to realize that points are not always given in life. I question the motivation behind the games and points.

Reaction

Linda Dmytriw (Teacher Trainee)

I absolutely agree that a credible discipline system meshes with one's personality. Put mundanely once again, classroom management does boil down to "whatever works." And to find out what "whatever" includes, we must always be open to new options. As a language teacher, one of my goals is to provide my students with a relaxed, low-stress learning environment. I also know that a certain amount of tension and pressure are necessary for students to take academic performance seriously. Group work guised as games has been very successful for my intermediate ESL students yet not as popular with my "regular" English students. I have other devices and gimmicks for them.

I tend to use rather authoritarian methods such as those suggested by the trainee's mentor (except for rule #4), and I find that they actually help me to create an atmosphere of fun and excitement. I use a point system to keep noise and inappropriate behavior to an absolute minimum. In fact, during group work, discipline problems are for all intents and purposes annihilated. If someone dares "breathe too loudly," I deduct a point from his or her team. For me, point systems are only successful as long as I provide an immediate material reward such as stickers for the group banner or candy. One reason I restrict group work to no more than two hours a week (a block ESL class meets two hours a day) is that the kids like it too much. There are, of course, other reasons.

In my two years of public school teaching in L.A., I have also seen that men and women often have to employ different tactics for managing their classes. Whereas boys in my school would not actually hit a female teacher (too macho for that), I do think they might strike a male teacher — especially if he were as abrasive as I find I need to be in order to keep respect and order in class. Essentially, I am a soft and yielding person but I try not to expose this side of my personality unless it is well protected. I learned quickly that certain students have a nose for vulnerability.

Because so many students challenge our methods and teaching objectives every day, we must individually find a means of coping with any number of social problems as well as of delivering quality instruction. Teachers are not threatened by robots or computers. The real threat is burn out. It seems to me that a continual refinement of management systems is our best antidote to premature retirement, burn out, or — God forbid — excessive public humiliation.

Reaction

Patricia Norton (Experienced Teacher)

It is impressive that the new teacher who wrote this vignette stumbled onto so many solutions to the problems he faced — and so soon! I know many experienced teachers who have not as yet discovered the advantages of cooperative learning

techniques, positive reinforcement, and simplifying routines. His willingness to risk trying new tactics showed a fine determination.

Had I been his mentor I would hope that I would have recognized that my initial suggestions about how to handle the discipline were not appropriate for him and his personality and could have helped with other methods that he found more comfortable. I am concerned about the reason he found it more desirable to rely on another new teacher instead of his mentor. There was no mention of evidence of improved learning with the advent of his new techniques. As a mentor, I would have been interested in examining that aspect with him also. It is possible, however, that the mentor teacher recognized that he was the type who benefited most from exploring techniques on his own until he found those that suited him and his students best.

I am not sure that I wholeheartedly agree with his concluding statement, "I believe it doesn't really matter what specific methods a teacher used to instruct and discipline his students. The key lies in finding a serious yet credible system that meshes with one's personality." I think there are some proven specific techniques out there that are worthy of trying. It takes some effort, research, and use of resources to discover these strategies, but they are available. As it stands, his statement might also conclude that bashing students over the head would make a nasty-dispositioned teacher credible to his students! We, as teachers, are here to help students learn, not necessarily to put across or pamper our personalities. Perhaps he meant to indicate that teaching should not be restricted to a formula, but that success is possible with many different approaches to the same curriculum. I am in total agreement with this conclusion.

Reaction

Donna Colbert (Experienced Teacher)

As a veteran of an inner-city senior high, I can understand this trainee's dilemma. It is not easy trying to decide which style of discipline is the best. If a particular method is not working for you, then you should ask other teachers what they do. Or, if possible, observe other teachers' classrooms. This new teacher discovered the right blend for him. Through experimentation he found a style that was suitable to his needs. It sounds like all his exploration was not successful, but he kept trying until something worked and his classroom seemed less stressful.

I feel that the reason one type of discipline works for some teachers and not others is because of the various teachers' personalities. I have observed classes that I felt were in total pandemonium but I knew that the teacher had complete control. You could see the students learning, asking questions, and generally staying on the assigned task. The observed teacher was not bothered by the noise and moved freely throughout the classroom.

I agree with the trainee's assumption that "it doesn't really matter what specific methods a teacher uses to instruct and discipline his students. The key lies in finding a serious yet credible system which meshes with one's personality." I would like to place emphasis on the words "serious yet credible." Teachers are professionals. I feel that they are responsible enough to experiment with various types of disciplinary techniques and not revert to violence. It they cannot restrain themselves, then they should not be in the classroom.

It is up to the teacher to explore and experiment with new methods. Read the literature and try new ideas that may work for you. Even your well-thought style can be wrong for a certain class or for a new teaching assignment. The whole point of a proper disciplinary technique is to make your teaching experience less stressful and create a successful learning environment.

Reaction

Jere Brophy, Michigan State University

I am impressed by the image of the teacher that I glean from reading this case, but I disagree with his conclusion. Although it is true that a teacher must establish credibility and should feel comfortable with his or her own approach to teaching, it is also true that research has established that certain methods of teaching and managing students are more effective than others. Particularly in the case of classroom management, work by several teams of investigators located in different parts of the country and studying at different grade levels and in different types of schools (reviewed by Brophy, 1983, and Doyle, 1986) has produced replicated findings that converge on the conclusion that teachers who approach classroom management as a process of establishing and maintaining effective learning environments tend to be more successful than teachers who place more emphasis on their roles as authority figures or disciplinarians. Effective classroom managers arrange the physical environment of the classroom so that it is suited to the nature of the planned instructional activities, establish general expectations and rules at the beginning of the school year, establish routines for getting each class period started and ended and for managing transitions between activities, keep group activities going once they are started by stimulating student involvement and by intervening only in brief and nonintrusive ways (if possible), give clear directions for and assist in getting their students started on assignments, and attempt to meet the needs of individual students during times when attention can be diverted temporarily from instructing or supervising the work of the class as a whole.

The classroom management systems used by these teachers focus on establishing the classroom as an effective learning environment and include emphasis on maximizing the time that students spend actively engaged in worthwhile academic activities as well as accountability systems designed to ensure active participation in lessons and discussions and careful and timely completion of assignments. Thus, these teachers take their roles as instructors seriously, challenge the students, and aspire to do more than "keep it simple, fun, and entertaining," as Steinberg's friend and fellow English teacher puts it. The latter approach may indeed succeed in producing positive student attitudes toward the teacher and the class, but this "bargain" may be achieved only at significant cost in the extent and quality of the learning experience of the students (see Sedlak, Pullin, Wheeler, & Cusick, 1986, for extended discussion of this problem).

Although the best classroom managers make demands on their students, they are not lion tamers, as the mentor teacher in this case study suggests. They approach classroom management as involving primarily *instruction* (clearly articulating and explaining the reasons for rules and expectations; demonstrating and providing reminders about procedures and routines) rather than *discipline* (catching and punishing rule breakers). Their emphasis is on maximizing the time that students spend engaged in worthwhile academic activities and minimizing the time that they spend waiting for activities to get started, making transitions between activities, sitting with nothing to do, or engaging in misconduct. Their methods work not only in the sense that these teachers elicit student cooperation and intervene effectively when necessary, but also in the sense that they establish effective learning environments in which students are actively engaged in academic activities and are not merely under control. These teachers seek to minimize confrontations with students rather than win them over, and they begin smiling on the first day of school rather than waiting

REWARD SYSTEMS

until Christmas. Steinberg apparently developed an intuitive understanding of much of this; good teacher education programs cover it systematically enough so that their graduates do not have to learn it the hard way. (For scholarly reviews of this work see Brophy, 1983, and Doyle, 1986, and for applications see Emmer et al., 1984, Evertson et al., 1984, and Good & Brophy, 1986, 1987.)

My comments on contract points systems made in response to the "Expletive Somewhat Deleted" case apply here, as well. However, it appears that Steinberg was manipulating the point system effectively, given that the students not only were completing assignments but were participating actively in discussions and completing essays in addition to worksheets. His streamlining and conventionalizing of the classroom management system, described in the last paragraph of the case, is typical of teachers who experiment with contract point systems. Many teachers abandon them altogether, finding that the benefits do not make up for the costs in money spent for prizes, time and trouble spent keeping score and handling paperwork, and class time lost from lessons and used for awarding prizes. Many others, like Steinberg, retain certain aspects of the approach. For most such teachers, contract point systems eventually become mere supplements to, rather than the heart of, their basic approach to classroom management as they discover the general principles reviewed in Brophy, 1983, and Doyle, 1986.

The fundamental and important aspects of contract point systems are an emphasis on the positive (students are given guidance concerning what to do rather than merely warned against misbehavior, and they are rewarded for their efforts) and clarity concerning what will be required and on what basis credit points will be allocated. Good teachers build these elements into their classroom management system, whether or not it includes a formal contract points system. Such systems, and the gimmicks associated with them, are often helpful to inexperienced or struggling teachers who have not been taught effective classroom management principles. Such teachers can lean on contract points systems temporarily as crutches to buy them time to develop effective rules, routines, accountability systems, and the other elements of an effective classroom management system through trial and error. They can then streamline or discard the contract points systems when they are no longer needed.

I noted that Steinberg used team competition as part of his approach. Such competition can be an effective motivation device, especially for routine practice tasks calling for mastery of particular knowledge or skills and when conditions are arranged so that each team has an equal chance to win. Teachers interested in team competition should familiarize themselves with the work of Robert Slavin (1983). He has developed methods that combine competition between teams with cooperation among members on the same team who tutor one another, administer mastery tests, and otherwise assist one another in learning the content in preparation for a competition to be held at the end of the week. Conditions are arranged so that all of the students have equal chances to earn points for their respective teams: they compete either against other students of similar achievement level or against individualized standards based on their own recent achievement records. Since each individual member must do well if the team is to achieve a high total score, team members are motivated not only to work toward their own personal mastery of the material, but also to help their teammates master it. These student-team learning methods have proven to be especially effective as alternatives to traditional individual seatwork in mathematics in grades 4-8, not only for supporting student achievement gains but also for improving the levels of positive feeling and prosocial interaction among students who differ in sex, race, ethnicity, achievement level, or handicapping conditions.

Steinberg notes that even under the point system, some students "simply did not choose to participate in any way." Rather than wait indefinitely for them to come around, I would "go after them" by calling on them to answer questions whenever they raised their hands and frequently even when they did not (especially when I had good reason to believe that they could answer the question successfully). In addition, I would schedule private conferences with such students in order to communicate my concerns. As a teacher I need feedback — when they remain passive I have no way of knowing whether they are attending and following the lesson. In addition, I value and desire their input to discussions and I would like to be able to answer questions or respond to comments that they might have about the content. I would also question them to find out if there is any particular reason why they do not participate, and would attempt to meet any need or respond to any problem that they expressed in response to this question. Before concluding the conference, I would attempt to negotiate commitment from the student to a particular goal (such as volunteering to respond to at least one question or making at least one contribution to a discussion each day).

Steinberg had already developed many important insights about effective classroom management at the time that this case was written. Still missing, however, is clear recognition of the intimate relationships between effective classroom management and the quality of instruction, as well as the recognition that an effective classroom management system is not an end in itself but a means for establishing the classroom as an effective environment for teaching and learning. There are hints in the case that Steinberg was beginning to recognize this intuitively (e.g., he streamlined and conventionalized his management system the next year). As he articulates these insights more clearly, his classroom management effectiveness as well as his instructional effectiveness should become even better.

References

Brophy, J. (1983). Classroom organization and management. *Elementary School Journal, 83,* 265-285.

Doyle, W. (1986). Classroom organization and management. In M. C. Wittrock (Ed.), *Handbook of research on teaching* (3rd ed.). New York: Macmillan. (pp. 392-431).

Emmer, E., Evertson, C., Sanford, J., Clements, B., & Worsham, M. (1984). *Classroom management for junior high teachers*. Englewood Cliffs, NJ: Prentice-Hall.

Evertson, C., Emmer, E., Clements, B., Sanford, J., & Worsham, M. (1984). *Classroom management for elementary teachers*. Englewood Cliffs, NJ: Prentice-Hall.

Good, T., & Brophy, J. (1986). *Educational psychology: A realistic approach* (3rd ed.). New York: Longman.

Good, T., & Brophy, J. (1987). *Looking in classrooms* (4th ed.). New York: Harper & Row.

Sedlak, M., Pullin, D., Wheeler, C., & Cusick, P. (1986). *Classroom perspectives on school reform*. New York: Teachers College Press.

Slavin, R. (1983). *Cooperative learning*. New York: Longman.

24 Hours: A Study of Perseverance

Leila Brandt

My first teaching assignment in the Los Angeles Unified School District was at Durney Senior High School. The school is comprised of primarily minority students. The area is poor and crime-ridden. Many of the students come from single-parent homes that are supported by AFDC (Aid to Families with Dependent Children). I was assigned to teach 9th and 10th grade English.

When I began at Durney I was 32 years old. I made a career change to teaching after having stayed at home with my children for three years. I had been a purchasing agent before beginning my family. I no longer wanted the pressures and long hours of that job. Teaching seemed an ideal alternative. Language and literature had been lifelong loves.

I began my teaching career working as a substitute teacher in the Compton Unified School District and then the Lynwood Unified School District. I enjoyed this very much, especially working at Lynwood High School, and I decided to pursue a full-time position. This pursuit lead me to the Los Angeles Unified School District, the Teacher Trainee Program, and finally, Durney Senior High School. Compton and Lynwood are minority communities, and I had functioned fairly well there. I didn't think any situation could be much worse. I was wrong.

My first experience at Durney was at a new teachers' meeting held on the day before teacher orientation. The talk was supportive. Help was promised. We asked who our mentors were. We were told they would be assigned later. They asked what we needed to start day one. I said I needed to be able to make copies. Paper and supplies were promised. These turned out to be false promises.

My greatest difficulty at Durney was getting past the head of the my department. She was also a mentor teacher and generally a very powerful person in the school. In a meeting or in front of an administrator, she offered everything. Getting anything from her was a different matter. I asked her to assign books to me from the first day. She refused and insisted that I had to have a meeting with the other teachers teaching the same classes to divide up what books were available. In the end, it took almost three weeks to get any books. When I asked for paper to make copies, I was told there wasn't any and I would have to wait. It took a week to get a pen from her.

I started my first day at Durney with no books, no copies and no supplies. That week I winged it, having the students copy off the board. They wrote dictations, sample essays and took spelling pretests. By the middle of the second week, I was beginning to panic. I approached the department chair and asked for a set of dictionaries. I figured that as an English teacher I was at least entitled to that. With dictionaries I could work on vocabulary and related skills until I got some paper or books. My request met with only negative results. She informed me that it was my failure as a teacher that made me feel I needed dictionaries to work on vocabulary, and that I would have to wait until she got around to distributing them. This was from a so-called mentor teacher! I still did not have my own mentor. At that point I called a mentor that I had met during the summer. She sent me some paper and supplies. I brought ditto books, and my students worked on those dittos until she got around to signing book cards and distributing dictionaries.

By the fourth week, I had managed to get most of what I needed. Then she assigned a mentor to me. At that point, I felt as if I had fought my own battles, that no one at that school was concerned or helpful, and that I didn't need a mentor. My mentor was in a different department anyway, and I didn't know who he was. He made no effort to make contact right away and I didn't bother.

It is hard to describe the shock I experienced during my first weeks of school. [As I saw it,] many students were loud, vulgar, poorly dressed and many had obvious physical problems, such as extremely crooked teeth, which in almost any other environment would have been taken care of by doctors. My heart went out to these kids, but at the same time they made me very angry. Every day I tried to get control of my classes. Every day it was an effort. Let me describe a typical day for me at Durney High School.

First period began at 8:00 a.m. Very few students were on time. They straggled in, a few at a time, throughout the class. It wasn't until they started a tardy lock-out policy in the fourth week that we had an uninterrupted class. Many students were locked out on a daily basis. I *followed* all the school policies to deal with habitually tardy students. They didn't work. I made phone calls. Most students' phones were disconnected. I talked with parents whose voices were slurred. It appeared to me that they had trouble following the conversation as if they were under the influence of drugs or alcohol. Some parents expressed deep concern and stated a willingness to get these kids in line, but the behaviors too often didn't change. When

I called back all I got was the same promises. I gave students written warnings, then detention, and then referrals. All of this took a great deal of my time both in and out of class, and it did no good.

Third and fourth periods were two of a kind. Out of each class of approximately 35 students, two to four were excellent and attentive, six to eight were mild talkers and tended not to do any work, and eight to ten were active talkers and disruptors who were determined not to do any work of any kind. The remainder were habitually absent. It was the active disrupters that I spent all my time and energy trying to control. In these classes, it was not enough to have a planned lesson and begin class. It was a contest to get them into their seats and then to get them to be quiet enough to begin. At this point, there were still problems. The majority of the students did not have basic materials with them, i.e., paper and pen. Theft was also a continual problem among students. Those students who did try to bring the required materials often had them stolen.

I covered as much of the course materials as possible with the time I had. It was difficult because many students were at second- or third-grade levels. No homework could be assigned because there were no books for them to take home. The discipline problems appeared great, and they were. I tried every discipline strategy that I encountered from any source. Conferencing with students didn't work. Phone calls home didn't work. Assigning detention didn't work. Even so, I continued a daily, aggressive discipline plan.

Fifth and sixth periods were my time to relax. Very few students showed up, only the few that were trying. These classes were my time to make an attempt at teaching. The habitual absences and truancies took a lot of my time outside of class doing follow-ups.

I began each class with a written dispatch. I used that time to take attendance and write referrals. I averaged three per class a day, mainly for unserved detentions. After that I gave them simple seat work. It had to be simple because lecturing and discussion were almost impossible. Even the simplest work was extremely difficult for many. I circulated constantly and worked with students on an individual basis. I don't pretend that I was doing any real teaching at that point because I wasn't. I was practicing crowd control at best.

I also began to have personal problems related to school. I came home at night extremely tense and upset. I did not allow myself to think about school. I would sit down, watch TV and try to escape. It didn't work. I began to have trouble sleeping. I took sleeping pills for awhile but then stopped because I felt worse. I took days off just to try to get some rest. I considered quitting. I finally began to practice a series of relaxation techniques. These helped and made it possible to continue working.

During this time, I had a great deal of help from outside resources. There was a retired teacher who came in weekly to observe and give advice. He wasn't much help because he would end up yelling at these kids, too. His final opinion was to work on getting rid of the worst ones. I also had advisors from the Senior High School Division who visited regularly. They gave me a lot of encouragement. They usually left a written observation report with suggestions. It was done in a very positive manner and helped a great deal. My mentor was nowhere to be seen. He came and observed me once when I knew his mentor log was due. I threw his notes in the trash without looking at them.

I tried everything I could think of, but nothing worked with the discipline problems. I knew that there was no way I could really teach these kids until I licked those problems. One advisor from the Senior High School Division had been in to observe on a regular basis. He had given me many suggestions, but none had helped very much. He had admitted to me that these students were a tough group.

One day my advisor suggested some kind of reward system. It was during a meeting after he had observed the class, noting their attention span. He pointed out when I had them, when I lost them, and so forth. He had been in the class many times, and the subject of their emotional maturity came up. He came up with the idea of a reward system. We discussed it at some length. The next day he sent some books to me with suggestions. I thought it seemed too childish but at that point I was ready to try anything.

After giving it some thought, I came up with a reward chart. Each student's name was listed. At the end of each class, if the student had been on time, had been quiet, had materials, had worked on class assignments and had stayed seated, he or she received a sticker. Stickers were awarded in the last two to three minutes of each class. If the student had an infraction, it was noted on the chart. There were no warnings. One offense meant no sticker, two meant detention, three meant a referral. If a student had a "perfect week," he or she received an award on Friday. The reward was a simple ditto sheet worth one excused tardy, one excused dispatch, or 20 points on a class assignment or test. Twenty points were not very much.

The classes turned around overnight. The first few days were a little rough — mostly because the students couldn't bear not to get a sticker, and they were having a hard time changing their behavior patterns. Students looked forward to the end of class when the stickers were awarded with great anticipation. Students loved that little bit of tangible recognition. On Friday, the awards were a minor celebration. Many awards were taken home and never traded in.

This system had a few failures. Three students just couldn't buy into it and ended up getting put out of class or just never coming anymore. They continued to act as they had before, only now their behavior stood out like a sore thumb instead of being at the forefront of a general commotion.

I don't want to make it sound like everything was now perfect. It wasn't. But for the first time I had classes that were trying to participate. Now I began real lesson preparation. We had our first class discussions. It was difficult because the students really didn't know how to behave in a regular classroom situation. It was as if for the first time they were trying. I still had problems, but only one or two. Now I had the opportunity to begin to teach.

I feel that the reason this worked at all is that these students are the products of failures in education. They had never done well. They had never been rewarded. Consequently, they didn't care about their behavior or anything else connected with education. My system gave them a small reward. It was an immediate reward. It had visual representation both in the chart, which was prominently displayed in the classroom, and in the weekly awards.

I would like to share one success story. There was one Hispanic student who was real trouble. He broke almost every rule in class imaginable. He was in trouble with the dean on a regular basis. He had a very hard time adapting, and I had just about given him up. Then, about nine weeks into the system, a miracle happened. He earned a perfect week award. I was surprised. The other students were, too. When I called out his name and he walked up to get his award, the other students burst into spontaneous applause. That kid had an expression on his face that I had never seen before. He looked shy and happy and proud. Gone was the tough, street-smart, wise-mouth lad. Instead I saw the sweet young man that hid under the hard exterior. He was the only student to win such applause. He never had another perfect week, but his behavior did continue to improve.

At the end of the fall semester, I lost my position at Durney due to lack of enrollment. I had extremely mixed feelings about leaving. It seemed as if all my hard work was going down the drain, but at the same time it was a chance to escape. On my last day at Durney, my students organized a surprise party for me during lunch. It included chips and punch as well as little presents. This was all at the student's expense and highly unusual for this school. They said I had been their best teacher. I was very touched. I began to feel that all my difficulties had been worth it.

Reaction

Don Kemper (Experienced Teacher)

This new teacher found a way to express the frustration, the stress, the emotional drain, the loneliness, and the powerful love encountered by all teachers in the inner city. Her vignette made me cry! In a single semester, she discovered, more or less by herself, that the real successes come one child at a time, and that teachers must consider the uniqueness of each child as we teach. Her students obviously held her in as high regard as I now do.

I got a very real sense of a woman with confidence in herself and the emotional strength to back it up. I feel guilt by association that she did not have a mentor to lean on. I cannot help but wonder how wonderful her first semester might have been if she had been paired with a compassionate and knowledgeable mentor at the new teacher meeting before school opened. When will we, in this emotionally draining profession, learn to have compassion for each other? I wonder if she had neighbors up and down the hall that were even rooting for her. Thursday classes at the Professional Development Center must have been extremely important to her, sharing her anxiety and stress with others who could sympathize.

We all can learn a lesson from this teacher. She displayed the ability to analyze what was occurring in her classroom and to make changes and to continue to make changes until she discovered something that worked. She was open to advice and used the small amount of help that was offered in productive ways. It must be remembered that the idea of positive reinforcement came from someone else, but this teacher worked out the details that made it succeed.

She spoke for all of us who care when she described the simple party of chips and punch and little presents, comprehending that it was a special and unusual effort, and realizing after all, that even her extreme difficulties had been worth it.

Reaction

Susan Taira (Experienced Teacher)

While I appreciate the new teacher's situation, I have struggled with my response because of my objections to the writer's narrow view of her initial contact with the students and the parents. It is my opinion that her statement on this view fosters segregation and discrimination, even though I am sure that it was not the writer's intent. The students and parents of any community deserve a fairer picture than the one described here.

My concern is also related to the teacher's projection of all problems to outside sources rather than taking some of the responsibility. Our difficulties as beginning teachers are due in part to our inexperience and lack of knowledge. We can be as imperfect as the writer views others.

I agree with the teacher's discovery about human nature, which is that we can foster a change in behavior through positive reinforcement instead of negative systems. It also puts us in a proactive position rather than a reactive one.

Reaction

Pam Grossman, University of Washington

In reading this new teacher's story, I am struck with the power of her honesty in describing her experiences at Durney High School. Her honesty, if brutal at times, allows us to more clearly see the extreme difficulties faced by teacher trainees and to begin to untangle some of the skills, knowledge, and understanding necessary for new teachers to succeed in the classroom.

While Ms. Taira objects to the teacher's initial impressions of her students and their parents, what the teacher describes could well be evidence of culture shock. This teacher has entered a world and culture that differ dramatically from the one in which she was evidently raised; the disequilibrium she experiences as a result of this conflict of cultural norms and expectations could be all the more debilitating because it occurs in her own country and in the all-too-familiar institution of school. While Ms. Brandt may have leaped to hasty and possibly faulty assumptions about the students and their parents, it is too easy to condemn her responses.

The culture of teaching is already too impatient with beginning teachers' stories of struggles and lack of success. Instead, we should welcome her account, accepting the feelings while challenging possible misconceptions, as an opportunity to rethink how we prepare, or fail to prepare, new teachers for culturally diverse classrooms. By explicitly preparing teachers for the school cultures they will enter and by helping them understand the realities and perspectives of the students and their community, experienced teachers and teacher educators alike can help ease entry into an unfamiliar world and challenge the misconceptions new teachers may rely on to explain the unfamiliar. What is admirable is this teacher's perseverance and her evident success in working through her initially negative impressions to establish a truly caring relationship with her students.

This teacher's story also makes us aware of the difficulties new teachers encounter when they begin teaching without a clear framework for conceptualizing the goals and subsequent strategies for teaching their subject matter. Ms. Brandt's evident discomfort with the idea of beginning teaching without a textbook is certainly understandable. Her feeling, however, also illustrates the extent to which she, like many new teachers, relies on curriculum materials to supply both her lessons and her objectives. Her story of planning to teach vocabulary suggests materials in search of a purpose. Her initial plans are governed by the structure of worksheets and dictionaries; her purposes in using these materials are less evident.

If we are going to send new teachers into classrooms without even the familiar prop of textbooks, which at least provide some rudimentary framework for the thinking about how to sequence and present subject matter for teaching, we must certainly help them develop a clear framework for thinking about the purposes and goals for teaching a subject, a map for where they plan to head with their students, and an understanding of the alternative routes they might use to get there. Without such a guide, new teachers can all too easily get lost in a maze of worksheets and borrowed materials.

Reaction

Jere Brophy, Michigan State University

The contrast between this case and "Expletive Somewhat Deleted" is striking. Brandt not only did not receive extra support and assistance from the school administration and mentor teacher, she did not even receive basic equipment and supplies. The school sounds like it had serious problems in administrative leadership and staff morale, two key factors in school effectiveness (see Good & Brophy, 1986, for a review of the school effects research).

Brandt's response was mixed. On one hand, she overracted to the problems and made things tougher on herself than they had to be. She could have purchased cheap pencils and paper to use until supplies arrived, and she never gave the assigned mentor teacher a chance to be helpful. On the other hand, she persisted despite serious external obstacles and her own self-described personal problems until she eventually achieved noteworthy success.

Here is another case where installation of a rewards system made a big difference in student response to the class. The comments I made about contracts, points and rewards systems in my reactions to "Expletive Somewhat Deleted" and "The Points" apply to "24 Hours" as well. I suspect that if she had stayed in this school, Brandt would have adjusted her reward system to base it on assigned points rather than stickers and to place relatively more emphasis on earning points through good lesson participation and work quality, not just avoidance of disruptive misbehavior. Even so, the system seems to have worked rather effectively for the time it was in effect.

Brandt's concern for her students comes through in her case report, and the going away party that the students staged for her suggests that it came through to the students, too. What does not come through, however, is her stated life-long love for language and literature. Practically nothing is said about the content of the instruction; and the references to "written dispatches" and low-level seatwork make the class sound dull and lifeless even when the students were cooperative. If the picture of this teacher and her classes that I gleaned from reading her case is correct, her difficulties lay as much in student motivation as in classroom management. She needs to become more effective in modeling and communicating her enthusiasm for the subject matter, and to learn about and use motivational strategies such as stimulating student interest and curiosity, linking the content to the students' life experiences or current interests, and stimulating their motivation to learn (see Brophy, 1987, and Good & Brophy, 1987, for discussion and examples of motivational strategies).

She is aware that students need to feel confident, that they can achieve success with reasonable effort before they will be willing to invest such effort in an academic task; however, she seems much less aware that in addition to such confidence, students need to *value* the task — to see it as interesting or enjoyable, or at least to recognize its importance and to want to learn the knowledge or skills that it is designed to develop. The case gave no indication that the teacher was aware of the

need to stimulate and develop such motivation to learn in her students. Worse, she probably undermined whatever tendency the students may have had to see value in the work (the dispatch assignments, at least) by including release from responsibility for completing these assignments as part of her reward system. This has the effect of communicating to the students that such assignments are nothing but onerous busywork, when the teacher should be communicating to the students that assignments are well-planned learning opportunities that will help them develop important knowledge or skill and, of course, should follow through by offering assignments that conform to this description.

Another related suggestion that I might make regarding this case is that the teacher needs to come on strong to her students not merely as a concerned adult and classroom manager but as an *instructor*. The content and skills that she intends to teach are not only potentially interesting and enjoyable to learn but important to the occupational and social success and all-around quality of life of the students. She should try to make her students understand why the content and skills she teaches them are so important for them to learn — not so much negatively ("People will look down on you and won't want to hire you for good jobs if you don't speak, read, and write well.") as positively ("I'm concerned about you as individuals and about the quality of your present and future lives, so I am trying to help you understand why this is important for you to learn and not just something for you to do to get a grade on a report card.")

Finally, I noted that the teacher felt that she could assign only the simplest seatwork, and even then had to circulate constantly and help the students. Although her point about the very low abilities of many of the students in this class is well taken, it is possible (and in my opinion, likely) that the teacher was not preparing the students as well as she could have for these seatwork assignments before releasing them to work on the assignments independently. Not only research on classroom management but also research on relationships between teacher behavior and student achievement gain (reviewed in Brophy & Good, 1986) underscore the importance of designing and selecting seatwork assignments that are at the right level of difficulty for the students. Research also suggests the importance of going over the directions for the work and leading the class through some practice examples to make sure that they know what to do and how to do it before releasing them to complete the assignment on their own. If the material is new or confusing, or the class as a whole is exceptionally low in independent work skills, it may be more effective (as a teaching-learning device, not just as a classroom management device) for the teacher to lead the class in working through part or even all of an assignment rather than require students to work independently. Or, it may be appropriate for the teacher to get the majority of the students working independently and then form the least-able students into a small group and lead them through the assignment as a group exercise. Another alternative that might be used with some forms of seatwork is cooperative learning, in which students work together cooperatively in pairs or small groups, discussing tactics for responding to each item or problem, then working independently on it, then comparing answers and resolving any discrepancies through discussion and continued problem solving attempts. (See Good & Brophy, 1987, or Slavin et al. 1985, for discussion of such cooperative learning techniques.)

References

Brophy, J. (1987). Socializing students' motivation to learn. In M. L. Maehr & D. A. Kleiber (Eds.), *Advances in motivation and achievement* (vol. V). Greenwich, CT: JAI Press. (pp. 181-210).

Brophy, J., & Good, T. (1986). Teacher behavior and student achievement. In M. C. Wittrock (Ed.), *Handbook of research on teaching* (3rd ed.). New York: Macmillan. (pp. 328-375).

Good, T., & Brophy, J. (1987). *Looking in classrooms* (4th ed.). New York: Harper & Row.

Good, T., & Brophy, J. (1986). *Educational psychology: A realistic approach* (3rd ed.). New York: Longman.

Slavin, R., Sharan, S., Kagan, S., Hertz-Lazarowitz, R., Webb, C., & Schmuck, R. (Eds.) (1985). *Learning to cooperate, cooperating to learn*. New York: Plenum.

CHAPTER THREE
INTERACTIONS WITH TEACHERS

- *VERY HELPFUL*
- *HELPFUL*
- *USELESS*

The preceding two chapters focused on instructional events and interactions with students. Several teachers alluded to how other teachers influenced their ways of handling certain teaching situations. This chapter concentrates on those influences. The task was to describe any interactions with a mentor teacher, an administrator, or another teacher who made a real difference in the author's teaching. Alternatively, the author was to describe an interaction that was ineffective or even harmful.

Experienced teachers (e.g., mentors) can help newcomers in many ways. The list below identifies six major areas, beginning with the easist kind of assistance and ending with the most difficult.

- At the beginning of the year, mentors can help new teachers learn about the procedural demands of the school, such as attendance and grading procedures.

- Mentors can provide opportunities for teachers to observe themselves and other teachers so they have access to several kinds of models.

- Mentors can share their own knowledge about new materials, unit planning, curriculum development, teaching methods, classroom management, and discipline.

- Mentors can act as a sounding board for curriculum decisions, discipline problems, and moral support.

- Mentors can observe their colleagues in their classrooms and engage them in an analysis of their teaching. This process is called coaching.

All types of assistance are important parts of the mentoring process, but the last one represents the key to continuous learning. There is simply no substitute for seeing how real students respond to instruction and materials. No matter how experienced and talented they may be, teachers will be of little help to one another unless they can see each other at work with students.

Observing others, being observed, and talking about the observation holds the risk of hurt feelings, the risk that persons will offend one another. But the potential gain is increased understanding and learning, and improved practice. Teachers say that observation and feedback is an important source of information and advice.

Good mentors also actively listen to the concerns of their colleagues. They know how to accept their fears and do not hasten to assure teachers that what concerns them is inconsequential. Mentors know when to provide direct guidance, such as in the first few months of teaching, and provide praise whenever it is warranted. Good mentors also know how to engage their colleagues in a reflective analysis of their teaching, so they can continue to learn after they have passed the survival stage. It is this ability to reflect and learn that enables teachers to uphold high standards of teaching.

In the Los Angeles Unified School District, several individuals are available to help teacher trainees during the induction years. First, a mentor teacher is assigned to each trainee. In theory, mentors and proteges are matched by school site and content area. In reality, as we see in a few of the cases in this chapter, the matches are sometimes faulty. Second, in hard-to-staff schools, a program advisor is hired specifically to assist the new teachers. Other individuals at the school site who can provide assistance include department chairs, principals, and, informally, experienced teachers in the same content areas.

Overview of the Chapter

The cases in this chapter represent a continuum of assistance from "very helpful" to "useless." In the first two accounts, mentor teachers were on the "very helpful" side of the continuum. They were constantly available as a sounding board for ideas and moral support. They also shared ideas and materials, provided models of competent instruction, gave praise whenever it was warranted, frequently observed the neophyte's teaching, and provided useful feedback. The cases suggest that the mentor's written suggestions and oral feedback enabled the neophyte to reflect on his or her practice and learn from critical incidents.

The remaining cases describe a range of individuals who were both helpful and useless. The most helpful colleagues were those who came into the classroom to observe and give constructive feedback. "Useless" mentors either taught different content areas, and were thus limited in helping the newcomers translate their knowledge of the subject matter into relevant lessons, or introduced themselves as mentors but did not follow through by offering specific assistance. This lack of follow-through suggests that some sort of evaluation system for mentors beyond the existing mentor log is warranted.

The authors who wrote these cases were among the lucky few who received help from other colleagues when the mentors failed to do so. Teacher aides, department chairs, program advisors and other experienced teachers were among those who provided the necessary support. What comes through loud and clear from the cases is that without collegial support, these novices might have joined the multitude of teachers who quit teaching during their first year.

At the request of the authors, all cases in this chapter will remain anonymous. Additionally, no attempt was made to solicit reactions to these accounts.

VERY HELPFUL

Nestor to Abecedarian: A Mentor Case Study

From Homeric times, a *nestor* has come to mean a wise man who is respected for his age and wisdom. To coin a word, my mentor is not a nestor but a *nestora*. I am the abecedarian, one who is just learning, a novice. Together for two years we have made the voyage through the Teacher Trainee Program. My mentor was first introduced to me on my second day of school. She introduced herself. I was concerned that I might not have a mentor teacher at my school, and I was relieved to know that she was just around the corner. And I was always running around the corner. Even though I had previous teaching experience, this new high school setting was different. For one, the noise about drove me crazy! As I settled into my classroom (at least in my mind), I began to have hundreds of questions.

I would make every opportunity to visit my mentor for individual conferences to discuss questions and concerns I had. I always made sure that I asked her two to four questions from my list; my complete list would have overwhelmed anyone. I knew that she had her own work to do without my added excitement about things that, as she pointed out to me, would eventually become clear. I know she gets paid a king's ransom for mentoring and she owes me time. However, I wanted our professional relationship to be good so I did not, or I tried not to, act my usual hyper-self.

My mentor was always calm, cool, and collected. I hoped that some day I would act the same way to other teachers. It was comforting to know I could go to her with anything — question, concern, expression, or whatever — without her passing a value judgment upon me openly. I am sure there are times she found me a bit obtuse, a Prufrock teacher.

I think that when she came to observe my classes the first year, she got a better sense of me, and I, in turn, got a better sense of her. My comments were direct as were my questions. I feel that I was sincere with her. Sometimes I became angry about the students, myself, and others. These concerns, feelings, opinions, and values I openly expressed to her. I am glad I did. For whatever her personal opinion may have been — at times I did not know, yet sometimes I did — she never discouraged, hindered, criticized, or devalued me. If anything, she encouraged, coaxed, suggested, tempered, and modified my thinking. Here is an example from one of her notes:

10/28/85
10:30-11:30

1. Student comment—"He's got the class under control now." (Worth a thousand cheers!)
2. Good handling of seating chart
3. Your approach to class policies and to students was done *well*.

Now, you know I felt good. As I look through the stack of "Memo From…" I feel the impulse to record another example:

11/20/85
10:30-11:00

1. Good procedure for issuing books!
2. How is your new room arrangement working?
3. Good approach to students' oral reading — especially the young man who was having difficulties.
4. Students seem interested in the literature focus for today. At least they have ideas to share — important.

Now that you have read the positive, let me reveal some other interesting comments:

11/19/86
9:20-10:00

9:35 a.m. — More tact in speaking to female student openly — perhaps a quiet conference would be helpful.

10/21/86
9:20-10:00

Consider — you had better control of communication when you moved from behind the desk!

10/16/86
Period 3

Body language — When you moved to side of classroom (discussing Alexander Pope) some students seemed to become inattentive.

At times my mentor appeared overly protective:

4/10/86
9:10-9:35

Did you write a referral on the young lady who was so rude — or make a parent call?

My lists could go on and on. (By the way, is it surprising that I would have *saved* all these missives?) Let me bring you totally up to date:

3/16/87

As per our conversation this morning, the following strategy might be helpful:

1. Take some time to discuss general class decorum/rules with students
2. Parent contact
3. U's or unsat. notices
4. Counselor referrals

Be consistent in approach to management. Careful of voice.

After two days I was still making mistakes:

3/18/87 10:35-11:15

Suggestions:

1. Soften voice tone when displeased.
2. Possibly return papers at the end of class which would allow the start of instruction after the tardy bell.

The observations were astute and the comments were positive. I took my mentor's comments into serious consideration: I realized that she was beginning to know me. My voice is loud to begin with. I thought this was good because I should shout over the crowd. I see what she means.

My mentor was helpful to me. I am not sure I could have gotten along without her. She was there when I needed someone to talk to. She gave me time. I have no complaints against her; well, maybe just one: she never took me to dinner.

As I reflect on my three semesters of teaching, I cannot say that my mentor has given me bad advice. She knows the rules. She knows the students. She knows teaching. She knows experience. This makes her very credible to me as a mentor. Since we are both English teachers, we share some literary trivia — she tells me how well read I am, but I disagree — and we have a good time in our little world of literature.

After all the roll taking, five-, ten-, fifteen-, twenty-week grades, absences and tardies, two comments, bubbling [marking grades in the grade book], bubbling, and bubbling, and correcting papers, and correcting papers, and bubbling, and bubbling, and correcting more papers, making lesson plans, xeroxing, making lesson plans, revising lesson plans, and more bubbling and more papers to correct, I come full circle — like that bubble demon — to realizing that my nestora has helped me to escape my abecedarian class. Although I feel I will always be learning — as I know my mentor will always be learning from the next novice — her critical comments were essential to part of my success as a teacher.

I also think that personality deals a heavy hand in this type of relationship. I was lucky. All I can say is that I was sincere, vocal, and up-front with my questions. I believe my mentor respected me for this. I cannot help but feel that it annoyed her sometimes even though she did not show signs of irritation. As a matter for the record, I have seen her angry only once (not at me). Whenever she sees me mad, she says, "Now, now." This brings a reality to my emotional state.

I have indeed been fortunate to have such a caring, responsive, and wise mentor-mother. I still regret that she did not take me to dinner. On the other hand, maybe I will take her.

A True Mentor

The man assigned as my mentor teacher was not officially designated as such until September 1986, the beginning of my second semester as a teacher trainee. He had, however, performed all of the functions of a mentor from the first day of my assignment in September 1985. When I was first accepted into the Teacher Trainee Program I had already completed one semester teaching under an emergency credential. Since I was the only teacher trainee in Senior High Options, the district assigned me to the only active mentor in Options.* However, the mentor taught at another school, located approximately 25 miles from my high school. Under the best of traffic conditions offered by Los Angeles freeways, the trip from one school to the other takes no less than two hours. During that first semester, she made one trip to my school, and I made one trip to hers. The suggestions she offered and materials she shared were of significant value, but the distance between us was an obstacle which we mutually agreed would be overcome only at my specific request.

My true mentor provided me with daily assistance and guidance since the day I walked onto the campus of my high school. As far as I know, he did this for no other reason than that he saw a need and felt moved to fulfill it. He took a personal interest not only in my performance but in my well-being. He never let an opportunity pass to point out any success I was experiencing, no matter how small. If I were preparing to try something new, he first complimented me on my innovativeness, THEN he showed me the pitfalls. The positive always came first.

Because my principal had such confidence in my mentor, I had a built-in buffer from the school's administration and never felt any of the pressures so often thrust upon a new employee. Since we shared the same room, I always took my conference periods in the classroom while he was teaching. I had the opportunity to see what kinds of interpersonal approaches worked and which did not. Many of the students in his class were under the impression they had two teachers, when in fact there was an extra student, not an extra teacher in the class.

By the end of the first year, I began to diverge more and more from my mentor's style of teaching, and adapted the contract system to my own abilities. He never criticized me for failing to adopt each of his techniques. In fact, he frequently used lessons that I had developed. This clear demonstration of respect for what I was doing amounted to one of the most rewarding experiences of my first year of teaching.

* The Options division of Los Angeles Unified School District (LAUSD) includes the continuation high schools, opportunity high schools, and other alternative programs designed for those students who have been unsuccessful in the comprehensive, traditional school setting. There are 56 such schools within LAUSD.

VERY HELPFUL

What My Mentors Have Meant to Me

No one could have prepared me for that big change from graduate school student at San Francisco State University to junior high school English teacher in East L.A. The transition is a radical one, one that curdles the psyche and wrenches the soul. Academically, I was prepared for the job, but I had no classroom management skills nor previous experience with a seven-hour-a-day teaching schedule that included only adolescent kids. Although I'd taught English in South America for three and a half years, my students there had entered the classroom highly motivated. They knew what they wanted from life and why. They were mostly executives or of university age. However, my students were all ESL — Mexican and Central American. My expectations of cultural and linguistic similarities between my previous students and these "squirrely little children" were shot down and beaten to a pulp. By lunchtime, I was a mess.

I had students tell me they didn't know their own names. I believed them. They had me running in circles and bouncing off walls. They would have devoured me if Nena hadn't stepped in. Nena was technically my teaching assistant. She showed me how to mark the computer roll book, where the supplies were, how to get the plant manager's attention, and how to call the kids' homes. She told me when the kids were cursing and what it all meant. She said she understood my Spanish and so could they. Through her I got my bearings, regained a sense of calm, and viewed the total situation from a more realistic perspective. No, students in Mexico definitely weren't allowed to make animal noises in class. And if they did, they were immediately expelled . . . forever. In Spanish, _nena_ means "baby." My Nena weighed about 250 pounds. To me, Nena meant muscle and force. By February she and the kids threw me a surprise birthday party. From then on we all got along.

So my first and most valuable institutional mentor was really my teaching assistant. In all honesty I feel I have learned more from her than any other person. But after six weeks had passed, I was introduced to the first of three official mentors I was to have. And each gave me another form of insight and assistance.

Along about October, a tall, blond, youngish man in a suit walked into my room and introduced himself as my mentor. In the name of Madeline Hunter he interrupted my making out grades. I've forgotten his name so I'll refer to him as Peter.

He taught in another school and was working on his Ph.D. Once a week we met in the school cafeteria and discussed a chapter from Madeline Hunter's _Mastery Teaching_. He then formally observed my sixth-period intermediate ESL reading class every Friday.

Not only did I learn the seven-step lesson plan, but I learned how others reacted to "outsiders" who were newer than myself. Once Peter told me he had been so frustrated his first year of teaching that he smashed his fist through the file cabinet in his classroom. For the weeks that followed, my sixth-period class (a notoriously restless bunch) displayed exceptionally good behavior whenever Peter entered the room. On the days he observed, he sat in the left back corner of the class and silently took notes. I never told the students that Peter was there to observe _me_ and not _them_.

Although I have always felt uneasy about being observed and somewhat awkward in the presence of my "superiors," Peter's input was definitely helpful. On the one hand, I could have done without the strain of such formal observations. On the other hand, the behavior of my sixth-period class was so difficult I welcomed an objective observer — especially from another school. Peter introduced himself as a friend and I accepted him as such. I have always found small talk and letting down my hair about certain problems difficult, so even if Madeline Hunter's seven steps were used as an excuse to get at what was really bugging me, the content of that book is also valuable.

In a few months, Peter was assigned to a different school. I was assigned another mentor. This mentor, who also teaches at my school, has a personality and approach quite different from my own. She's nice. I've already become mean. Deep inside I think I'm just a dippy-hippy who wants nothing more than to be left alone and kick back. But that side of my personality won't survive in a classroom in East L.A. I've learned that diamonds come from coal only under pressure. And I'm willing to exert it if there's even the promise of something valuable underneath. These kids have a lot of potential but it must be cultivated and developed.

One of my mentor's themes was that she wanted to help but didn't know how. It's true that most of the materials she gave me I put aside for the following year, but somehow, just knowing that The System had provided me with a "professional friend" made me more comfortable in school. Also, I knew the next year I'd be teaching most of my courses through the

English department rather than the bilingual department. When this mentor was around my kids acted "normally." That is, talking, laughing, and messing around. She didn't seem to mind and I didn't either. I felt less self-conscious about delivering the perfect lesson than I did with my previous mentor. I think it was through her I began to feel part of the school family.

At the end of the school year the English department met at my mentor's house to discuss materials and curriculum for the following year. I too was invited. Although her husband, also a teacher at our school, wasn't present, I learned about their personal-professional lives by browsing through their books, walking in their gardens and listening to some records my mentor brought out. Their daughter, herself a teacher, babysat my kids as we discussed young adult novels versus the classics.

Until just a few months ago this teacher remained my mentor. Besides passing me all kinds of useful materials, she said — more than once — "Remember, you've got to save time for your family." Some of us need to be reminded of the obvious. When two other teachers at our school became mentors, she moved on and I was assigned my third mentor.

This third mentor has the room next to my first-period class, a room I use only for that period (my other classes are in another building). She teaches health and has her Ph.D. She's in charge of the VCRs and is as neat as a nun. A big woman, and I'm sure quite strong, she is a part-time police officer. Rumor has it she actually walks a beat when not working in the classroom. She's always joking with the kids and is very kind. I've also been told that she is the one who leaves the delicious homemade breads and cakes for teachers to snack on in the lounge. She hasn't formally observed me or asked for any of my time, but we always borrow her stapler and sometimes we talk just before class.

A few weeks ago I had to call for help to stop a fight that was taking place on the floor below. The whole situation was disturbing. The next day my mentor came and chatted with me for awhile. She suggested some "think fast" procedures and I calmed down. Like most people, I guess I have always felt uneasy around police, but in this environment, where violence is a potential problem, I appreciate the presence of someone professionally trained to deal with it.

During the vocational education unit of English 8, I found out my best writing student might like to become a police officer. My mentor has since taken him on a field trip to the police academy and counseled him about scholarships for college. Twelve years ago, in my more serious writing days, I would not have even dreamed that I would some day be sending my most talented student writer and critical thinker to a police officer for vocational advice. But life is full of twists and turns. It's for us to find guidance and wisdom whenever we can along the way.

In theory and practice, I think the mentor program provides for professional growth as well as for personal development. My mentors have been and continue to be one of the most valuable resources offered by the district.

Useless Mentors: Fact or Fiction?

My experience as a teacher trainee with mentors has been somewhat less than positive. I was assigned a mentor teacher at my school site. The mentor proved to be quite elusive and unavailable. I would see her sometimes from across the campus. She would politely ask how I was every so often. She never came to my classroom. My dealings with her were limited mainly to my occasional requests for her signature on teacher trainee class assignments and approval for one or two "mentor days" so that I could write my classes' finals. She did not seem concerned about how I was faring in the jungle that I call my first year teaching. To be fair, she was handling three classes and was new to the school herself. However, I did feel some resentment at this pseudo-service offered by the district.

Three other mentors followed in succession as titles and responsibilities changed in the administration. I found that my next on-site mentor (she started with me during my second year teaching) seemed quite concerned, and asked me frequently if I was all right or if I needed anything. She was also very sympathetic. The week I almost quit my job, she advised me to take a "mental health" day off. However, even this mentor never found her way into my classroom.

Currently, I have a new on-site mentor, plus one from another high school. The one at my school is about as useful as my first on-site mentor. I see her around campus, though she has never shown interest in my class or asked how I'm doing. The other mentor from a different school has been surprisingly helpful. He has been to my class for observations about three times (he's only been assigned to me for a few months), and has had conferences with me concerning my techniques, frustrations, and possible solutions. He has called me at home to ask how things are going. I appreciate his concern and his taking time to see me, especially after my previous experience with mentor teachers.

So how did I survive as a new teacher at a Chapter I school in the heart of Watts? Most of my support came through a Priority Staffing Program Advisor. I believe they are assigned only to "hard-to-staff" schools, which seems unfortunate, since being a new teacher is difficult *anywhere*. My advisor visited my class about two times a week, offered very helpful suggestions, conferred with me during many a lunch period, and called me at home to see how I was doing. Most importantly, he offered moral support the many times I was discouraged, often by sharing his own experiences and feelings as a new teacher. (He taught for 14 years!) This advisor, more than anyone else at the school or in the teacher trainee program, kept me from resigning that first year!

I feel that the mentor teacher program is beneficial in theory, but I can't offer a strong endorsement from my own experience with it. Perhaps mentor teachers have too many responsibilities to be of real service to new teachers. Perhaps they don't regard their job as important. (I can affirm, as a new teacher, that it is!) Perhaps they're not interested in making the effort to reach new teachers. Whatever the cause, I believe the mentor teacher program needs to be reevaluated. The district needs to ask how much this program is actually contributing to the support of new teachers. The answers may be discouraging now, but the program's weaknesses must be faced before any constructive changes can occur.

The Mentor Experience: Boon or Bane

Each new teacher in the Teacher Trainee Program was assigned a mentor teacher. Theoretically, the mentor is supposed to be a well-seasoned veteran who provides both expertise and moral support to the new teacher. Unfortunately, mentors are paired with their mentees by school-site location rather than by subject area or other critical criteria. It is a matter of simple chance whether or not any particular mentor is well suited to meet their mentees' needs.

I was originally paired with a female math teacher, although I am a male science teacher. While she was able to provide the much needed moral support, she was not able to help me in several other important areas. Even a cursory observation of classroom teaching techniques will reveal that male and female teachers generally relate to the class with different strategies. Females often use the motherly or sisterly approach. I find that for males, the strongarm approach is most prevalent. The hardcore problem students responded much better to behavior modification suggestions such as, "Do that again and it'll be the last time you do *anything* in here," than to drawing the student aside and offering, "You know, it really displeases me when you set fire to your desk." As a result, classroom management advice from my mentor was often ineffective.

Since my mentor had never taught science, she was unable to provide me with what I most needed at the beginning of my first semester — a few good lesson plans. Although I have an extremely strong background in the subject material I am teaching, it was difficult to translate this knowledge into short, simple lessons for scholastically handicapped students.

I was also desperately in need of classroom supplies. The school provided me with *nothing*! No tape, no stapler, no file cabinet, no paper . . . nothing! This, in my opinion, was a major oversight on the part of the district. "Support" personnel at the school, other than the mentor, were of no help in this area either. Administrators insisted that no supplies were available. In fact, school officials often caused more problems than they solved. The school secretary is so rude that I have learned to avoid her except for my monthly paycheck pick-up. My department chairperson refuses to send in supply orders. The attendance office takes great pleasure in berating teachers for even the smallest deviation from their policies, which change weekly.

The only saving grace throughout my initiation ordeal was that two teachers in my department went out of their way to provide assistance to me. They loaned me equipment, shared lesson plans, and evaluated problems I was having. Eventually, one of the two applied for mentor status and became my mentor.

In conclusion, I feel that the mentor program can be a very effective means of easing new teachers into the profession if it is used properly. Some foresight must be used when pairing the mentor with a mentee. If the district continues to form these pairs with no thought as to the individuals united, then many of these relationships are destined to failure in meeting their intended goals.

CHAPTER FOUR
IMPLICATIONS OF A CASE LITERATURE
BY TEACHERS

The Intern Teacher Casebook is Far West Laboratory's second volume of case literature by teachers. It serves as a partner to the first casebook, written by mentor teachers about their new role supporting novice teachers. The present book contains vignettes written by neophytes who were mentored by assigned experienced teachers. Each account is a three- to six-page snapshot of an event or series of events that occurred during the first few months of teaching. We call the vignettes "cases" when we make the theoretical claim that they are "cases of something." For example, "Breaking the Barrier" is a case of "teaching new concepts and skills," and "Painful Growth" is a case of an "interaction with students."

An additional feature is added to the cases in this book — multiple reactions from other teachers and/or educational scholars follow most vignettes. The reactions can be viewed as "layers of commentary," similar to that found in the scholarly volumes of the Jewish Talmud. The cases and their layers of commentary can be studied by teachers, teacher educators, and researchers to infer, extend, or test principles of practice (L. Shulman, in progress).

What do cases written by the teachers themselves add to the literature on teacher induction? Why not simply ask teachers to summarize what they had learned during their first few months of teaching? It would take less space and be less time-consuming to produce. Perhaps we can illustrate the argument for a case literature by listing some of the principles of practice that these neophytes learned from their initial experiences:

- Teachers must always plan carefully; management problems occur more frequently when lessons are spontaneous.

- Good lessons and classroom management are interdependent. Teachers cannot establish an environment conducive to learning without attending simultaneously to developing appropriate instruction.

- Teachers must transform what they know into relevant lessons for their students; students cannot be expected to learn in the same way as their teachers.

- Teachers cannot rely merely on textbooks to teach new concepts and skills. They must supplement the texts with additional materials and activities.

- Teachers must teach new concepts and skills in incremental steps, assigning practice tasks and assessing students' knowledge during each stage of a unit. This process is called teaching.

- Students need teachers who act as positive adult models, not other peers or friends.

- Beginning teachers should approach experienced teachers for help before tackling new units. Veterans' suggestions and foresight may prevent problems before they occur.

These principles are similar to those that are taught in most teacher preparation programs and inservice workshops for beginning teachers. Yet it is one thing for new teachers to be told these principles, and it is another for them to understand why these are important. Stated as bold propositions, the principles may be valid but they are also dull and hard to remember. Cases clothe principles with context, embedding them in settings whose detail and reflective content lend life and meaning to the propositions.

What makes these cases so compelling is the imagery evoked by detailed accounts of how new teachers learned these principles and reflected on their experiences. Who can forget the dramatic descriptions of the difficulties that these neophytes encountered as they struggled to develop both relevant lessons for their students and a classroom environment conducive to learning? The cases make it clear that these teachers do not merely want to survive in their classrooms. They are committed to providing meaningful lessons for their students and continued to adapt their instructional tactics after reflecting on their critical experiences.

Although our original intent for this casebook was to create a tool for teacher preparation and staff development, we found that the project also had a powerful impact on the authors of the vignettes. Like the praise offered by mentors who contributed to *The Mentor Teacher Casebook*, these teacher trainees uniformly praised the process of case writing. They noted that writing the vignettes provided an opportunity to reflect on their teaching and analyze the outcomes, a rare event in the hectic lives of teachers. Reliving some of their "horrendous" first-year experiences helped some see how much they had grown professionally since they had started teaching. Others appreciated the opportunity to share their mistakes with other novices and mentor teachers, so they could benefit from the experiences. The following are representative comments from the teachers who wrote this book:

> The writing process was difficult but rewarding. The time required to write and revise the vignette while teaching a full load was substantial, but I felt satisfied to record a significant occasion in my early teaching career. It was useful for me to stop, reflect, and write about my experience. This enabled me to learn a lot more about

the situation instead of having it slowly fade into history.

I found the preparation of the vignette of significant value because it caused me to reflect upon how much help I needed and how much I received. It served also as a reminder of how far I had come in such a short time. I thought of the mentors who would read it, and I hoped that they would better empathize with their mentees as a result of the reading. There was, as well, a cathartic effect as I detailed the frustration I felt in those early days of teaching. I would recommend the process of writing vignettes to all new teachers and demand the process of reading them for all administrators and mentors.

Before [this project] I hadn't stopped to truly evaluate my teaching. The writing project gave me an opportunity to do just that. My vignette about the unsuccessful lesson was particularly helpful. When I wrote that I told my class that we were going to read [a play] "because the curriculum guide said so," I was startled. I said it, but my postrealization was especially shocking. It made me aware that sometimes the classroom context is a place completely isolated from other customs and norms. Outside of the classroom, I could not envision myself saying something like that, and expecting my students not to question me.

Next Steps

With the completion of two casebooks by teachers, we at Far West Laboratory and Los Angeles Unified School District are convinced of the power of these cases as educative tools. Not only is case writing an effective tool for encouraging teachers to reflect on their practice, as is recounted above, but the cases themselves also provide the means for others to learn from their experience. Teachers, teacher educators, administrators, policymakers, and administrators from around the world have responded favorably to the casebooks, because of what they can learn from the insiders, the teachers who work every day in their classrooms.

We hope that other teachers and administrators will join us in producing their own casebooks. With the development of a professional case literature, all educators will have a chance to learn from one another. The following observation from one of the experienced teachers who reacted to several vignettes summarizes our thoughts:

> The casebook method seems to me a quiet revolution in teacher training. During my own teacher training (which I felt was excellent), I know that the most important aspect was the practical. What I and my fellow trainees wanted was the chance to air our own "horror stories" and successes, and to receive feedback on these situations. The opportunity for trainees to get the flavor of a variety of positive and negative teaching scenarios seems to offer the moral support and pedagogic training that developing teachers most need.

ANNOTATED BIBLIOGRAPHY

Borko, H. (1986). Clinical teacher education: The induction years. In J. Hoffman and S. Edwards (Eds.), *Reality and reform in clinical teacher education.* New York: Random House.

Borko explores teacher induction practices and programs that are consistent with the Research in Teacher Education (RITE) framework of clinical teacher education. The chapter describes some characteristics of beginning teachers and focuses on the importance of support for these novices by experienced teachers during the induction years. Formal programs, such as California's Mentor Teacher Program, which accompany stipends, increased recognition and responsibility, and release time, have potential for providing appropriate support. Several alternative models for providing assistance and a curriculum for the delivery system according to the RITE framework are presented in detail.

Carter, K., & Koehler, V. R. (1987). The process and content of initial year of teaching programs. In G. A. Griffin & S. Millis (Eds.), *The first years of teaching: Background papers and a proposal.* Chicago: University of Illinois.

The writers propose content and processes for first-year teaching programs based on the conception of teaching as developmentally cognitive, emphasizing understanding rather than performance. An effective program should represent teaching as a largely cognitive activity, reflect knowledge needs of the beginning teacher, and attend to the gradual process of learning to teach. Two specific curriculum features are described to supplement the general structure. First, the development of a case literature is necessary to illustrate teaching practices and provide teachers opportunities for active analysis and problem-solving. Second, the establishment of a system of networking is important to help teachers develop the sense of being part of an important cohort.

Feiman-Nemser, S. (1983). Learning to teach. In L. S. Shulman and G. Sykes (Eds.), *Handbook of teaching and policy.* New York: Longman.

Feiman-Nemser views learning as the central feature of teaching and sees all teachers as students. The first year is the critical year of teaching, determining whether a person will stay in the teaching profession and what type of teacher the person will become. Unfortunately, beginning teachers are typically left to their own devices to work things out in a sink-or-swim, trial-and-error fashion. They typically concentrate on "what works," and are likely to focus on what is necessary to keep the class under control or to get things done. However, a focus on "what works" may not be educative in the long run. Concentration on survival skills may encourage beginning teachers to explore only a narrow range of alternatives, and may prevent teachers from a commitment to keep on learning and to hold high standards of effective practice. The chapter suggests a program of collegial support for beginning teachers, accompanied by a school culture that supports learning from teaching.

Fox, S. M., & Singletary, T. J. (1986). Deductions about supportive induction. *Journal of Teacher Education, 37*(1), 12-15.

Current assessment-oriented induction programs focus on observable teacher behaviors. These authors contend that teaching skill competence is not sufficient to guarantee that new teachers will stay in the profession and will develop the attitudes and reflective skills necessary for an "expert" teacher. A comprehensive induction program should include provision for acquiring additional knowledge and instructional skills, opportunities for developing attitudes that foster effective teaching, assistance in recognizing the effects of isolation, and aid in integration of the new teacher into school and community.

Fuller, F. F., & Brown, O. H. (1975). Becoming a teacher. In K. Ryan (Ed.), *Teacher Education* (Seventy-fourth Yearbook of the National Society for the Study of Education). Chicago: University of Chicago Press.

The investigators identify four hierarchical developmental stages of new teachers' concerns: (1) preteaching concerns, (2) early concerns about survival, (3) teaching situation concerns, and (4) concerns about pupils. Teacher education as it stands does not address these concerns as they occur. Two methods are suggested to help satisfy the teacher's concerns about self (the first three types of concerns identified) and allow him or her to shift concern to their pupils. The first is to *change the context* of teaching so that concerns about self are "neither generated nor exacerbated by threat, conflict, powerlessness, and unreasonable demands" (p. 40). The second suggestion calls for the provision of materials, information, and experiences to resolve self-concerns.

Gehrke, N. J. (1987). On helping the beginning teacher. In G.A. Griffin & S. Millis (Eds.), *The first years of teaching: Background papers and a proposal*. Chicago: University of Illinois.

> The writer draws upon sociology, anthropology, psychology, linguistics, and education to propose the establishment of a helping community for new teachers. She recognizes the developmental process of becoming a teacher and suggests that keeping in mind the concepts of *beginnings* and *rites of passage* is necessary for effective helping. Help specific to each phase of the new teacher's adjustment should be available. Effective use of *indirect enabling* and *affirmation*, two specific forms of gift-giving help, are vital for the formation of a strong community.

Grant, C. A., & Zeichner, K. M. (1981). Inservice support for first-year teachers: The state of the scene. *Journal of Research and Development in Education, 14*(2), 99-111.

> New teachers evaluated the *formal, informal,* and *job-embedded* support they received during their training and beginning teaching. They perceived *meetings with future co-workers* (other teachers, administrators) to be the most helpful form of pre-assignment support. Perceptions of post-assignment support must be examined relative to the quality, frequency, and availability of the support. Teachers named *planning time* as the most helpful form of support after they had been placed. The teachers suggested that they would find the following forms of support helpful during the induction process: (1) information about specific curricula to be taught and institutional materials available, (2) information on general school procedures, and (3) more in-class assistance from other experienced teachers or principals.

Howey, K. R., & Simpher, N. L. (1987). The role of higher education in the initial year of teaching programs. In G. A. Griffin & S. Millis (Eds.), *The first years of teaching: Background papers and a proposal*. Chicago: University of Illinois.

> The authors call for a restructuring of the current organization of institutions addressing teacher induction programs. Through collaborative, integrative methods with schools, institutions of higher learning can play a significant role in assisting beginning teachers. The authors describe in detail several forms of assistance from institutions of higher learning. Among these are the provision of a model of induction activities mutually beneficial to mentors and beginning teachers that incorporates knowledge of classrooms, observation procedures, and supervision methods; and direction for needed research in how to proceed with providing assistance and enabling teachers to better learn to teach.

Huling-Austin, L. (1986). What can and cannot be reasonably expected from teacher induction programs. *Journal of Teacher Education, 37*(1), 2-5.

> This thoughtful article analyzes generic goals of induction programs in terms of their plausibility and limitations. The following are the goals thus evaluated: (1) to improve teaching performance, (2) to increase the retention of promising beginning teachers during induction years, (3) to promote personal and professional well-being of beginning teachers, and (4) to satisfy mandated requirements related to induction and certification.

Huling-Austin, L., Barnes, S., & Smith, S. J. (1985). *A research-based staff development program for beginning teachers* (R & D Report No. 7201). Paper presented at the annual meeting of the American Educational Research Association, Chicago, IL. (ERIC Document Reproduction Service No. ED 361 989)

> The authors warn against structuring induction programs around the assumption that the first year of teaching is always a traumatic experience. Induction should be flexible enough to respond to an individual's needs at the appropriate time and should offer preparation for future issues as well as current concerns. The need for increased collaboration among various organizations responsible for aspects of the induction process is emphasized.

Jensen, M. C. (1987). *How to recruit, select, induct, and retain the very best teachers*. Eugene, OR: ERIC Clearinghouse on Educational Management, University of Oregon.

> In the chapter on induction programs, Jensen first summarizes attrition rates and the rationale for supporting beginning teachers. Then the author focuses on new teachers' problems and presents three workable induction approaches: mentor teachers, increased supervision and training, and newcomer support groups.

Little, J. W. (1986). Teachers as colleagues. In V. Koehler (Ed.), *Educator's handbook: Research into practice*. New York: Longman.

This chapter examines issues of teacher colleagueship — what differences colleagues make, what teachers do as colleagues, and the necessity of supporting collegial activities. Little celebrates close, rigorous, enduring work among teachers on fundamental issues of teaching and learning, but cautions that such instances are rare in schools today. For teachers to work often and fruitfully together requires optimum conditions on all fronts: (1) demonstrated value placed on shared work; (2) opportunities for shared work prominent in the daily schedule; (3) a compelling purpose for working together and a sufficiently challenging task; (4) adequate material resources and human assistance; and (5) recognition for the accomplishments of individuals and groups working together.

McLaughlin, M.W., Pfeifer, R. S., Owens, S. O., & Yee, S. (1986). Why teachers won't teach. *Phi Delta Kappan, 67*(6), 420-426.

The issues most central to the health of the teaching profession have to do with the fact that some of our most talented teachers believe that they can't teach, and thus they won't teach. Teachers who won't teach either leave the profession or resign themselves to going through the motions of educating children. These teachers find the process of teaching frustrating, unrewarding, and intolerably difficult. Teachers and school districts need to plan jointly systematic professional development for teachers. An organizational response is particularly important for the induction of new teachers.

Merry, R. W. (1954). Preparation to teach a case. In M. P. McNair (Ed.), *The case method at the Harvard Business School*. New York: McGraw-Hill.

This article suggests strategies for teaching using the case method. The instructor must be thoroughly conversant with the case as a whole, must assess principal areas for exploration and discussion and devise key questions to stimulate discussion. The instructor needs to be able to anticipate student questions and gauge how to address those questions. For purposes of facilitating future use of the case, the instructor may find it useful to jot down notes soon after the class session, touching on matters which need correction and including these notes in a case folder to be reviewed before preparing a new case outline.

A nation prepared: Teachers for the 21st century. (1986). New York: The Carnegie Forum on Education and the Economy.

Fundamental changes in the internal life of schools hold the greatest promise for transforming teaching into a rewarding and attractive career, say the authors of the Carnegie report. The task force recommends the creation of a career progression for teachers that would culminate in a lead teacher position. Lead teachers would continue to teach, but they would also play a role in setting instructional policy and in providing supervision to neophytes.

Odell, S. J. (1986). Induction support of new teachers: A functional approach. *Journal of Teacher Education, 37*(1), 26-29.

The functional approach of analysis is characterized by observing how an induction program offers assistance to new teachers. Specifically, this entails recording what help is requested by new teachers and observing what aid is offered by support personnel in response to their perceptions of the needs of new teachers. The two primary needs were (1) to obtain information about the school district, and (2) to obtain resources and materials pertinent to the information to be taught. As the school year went on, the need for system information decreased, and the need for help with teaching strategies and the instructional process increased. The support needs of new-to-system teachers were not significantly different from those of the new teacher, with one exception: new teachers asked for more help with classroom management. The author notes with surprise that emotional support is perceived as important but less needed than help in obtaining resources and materials or in adapting teaching strategies.

Rauth, M., & Bowers, G. R. (1986). Reactions to induction articles. *Journal of Teacher Education, 37*(1), 38-41.

Rauth claims that more than a clear definition of effective teaching is necessary at this point in planning and implementing induction programs. What is needed is the development of rigorous standards and norms applicable to each certified teacher. She addresses the issue of mentor teachers and calls for greater standardization and increased use of objective criteria in the selection of mentor teachers.

This writer also calls into question the assumption that a mentor's evaluatory position threatens the intimacy and trust between the mentor and the beginning teacher. Rauth states that an induction program that serves the status quo should be discarded. A program should foster a "new vision of the teacher as an artisan rather than a technician" (p. 40). Bowers emphasizes that, all else aside, the main point of an induction program should be to ensure the success of the beginning teacher.

Rosenholtz, S. J. (1987). Workplace conditions of teacher quality and commitment: Implications for the design of teacher induction programs. In G. A. Griffin & A. Millis (Eds.) *The first years of teaching: Background papers and a proposal.* Chicago: University of Illinois.

The author describes a number of experiences which should be afforded the new teacher, the conditions of which may require fundamental changes in the organizational and social arrangements of some schools. For example, the teacher should not be initially assigned to the most difficult schools or the most difficult students. The teacher should be afforded a level of professional autonomy and discretion enabling him or her to make informative choices through participation in decisionmaking processes with administrators and colleagues. Clear goals must be set by administrators, colleagues, and beginners. Frequent evaluative feedback relative to these goals must also be provided. New teachers need regular encouragement and acknowledgement of their efforts and occasional advice. Opportunities for communication and observation with more expert colleagues must be available. New teachers should be encouraged to experiment with a variety of teaching practices but should be informed about schoolwide expectations in areas such as student conduct. Also, new teachers must be given opportunities to involve parents with their children's learning.

Shulman, J. (1987). From veteran parent to novice teacher: A case study of a student teacher. *Teaching and Teacher Education, 3*(1), 13-28.

This article presents a case study of a student teacher's adaptation to the role of a teacher and factors that influenced the adaptation process. The student teacher's development is traced through changes in her teaching, and related changes in the language with which she described her experiences.

Shulman, J. H. & Colbert, J. A. (1987). *Cases as catalysts for cases.* Paper presented at the annual meeting of the American Educational Research Association, Washington, D.C.

The authors describe their methodology for developing *The Mentor Teacher Casebook.* It discusses how they used research-based cases to stimulate the writing of personal cases by experienced teachers.

Shulman, J. H. & Colbert, J. A. (Eds.) (1987). *The mentor teacher casebook.* San Francisco: Far West Laboratory for Educational Research and Development; and Eugene, Oregon: ERIC Clearinghouse on Educational Management.

This volume contains vignettes written by mentor teachers in the Los Angeles Unified School District about their work providing assistance to beginning teachers and highlights issues that reflect the complexity of the mentor role. Chapter titles include: "The Process of Mentoring," "Mentors and Administrators," and "The Life of a Mentor."

Shulman, L. S. (1987). Knowledge and teaching: Foundations of the new reform. *Harvard Educational Review, 57*(1), 1-22.

The author asserts that a conceptualization of teaching as a cognitive process is the basis for effective reform. Teaching is comprehension and reasoning, knowledge and reflection. Shulman argues that the development of a knowledge base is crucial at this point and outlines a detailed plan to effect this goal. From philosophical and empirical study, he proposes a process model of pedagogical reasoning and action, including the following phases: comprehension, transformation, instruction, evaluation, reflection, and new comprehensions.

Shulman, L. S. (1986). Those who understand: Knowledge growth in teaching. *Educational Researcher, 15*(4), 4-14.

Shulman describes his conception of the knowledge base of teaching (described above). He also argues that the development of a case literature on teaching would help us to understand the knowledge base of teaching. While cases themselves are richly described events or sequences of events, the knowedge they represent is what makes them cases. Shulman elaborates on the advantages of case literature and case knowledge in the paper.

Silver, P. (1986). Case records: A reflective approach to administrator development. *Theory Into Practice, 25*(3), 161-167.

Case records are prepared by professional practitioners (e.g., member principals at the Center for Advancing Principalship Excellence). The records are in a standardized form, include quantitative and impressionistic information, and consist of three elements: the facts of the case at the outset, a plan of action, and the results of the action. They are available to researchers and practitioners and can serve a variety of functions, such as identifying successful and unsuccessful solutions.

Tomorrow's teachers. (1986). East Lansing, MI: The Holmes Group.

The group of education deans that has come to be called the Holmes Group is organized around twin goals: the reform of teacher education and the reform of teaching. Included is a call for the development of a differentiated structure for professional opportunity and a realignment of responsibilities for teachers and administrators.

Varah, L. J., Theune, W. S., & Parker, L. (1986). Beginning teachers: Sink or swim? *Journal of Teacher Education, 37*(1), 30-34.

The University of Wisconsin-Whitewater Teacher Induction Program focuses on six domains: planning, management of student conduct, instructional organization and development, presentation of subject matter, communication, and testing. The authors describe this program in terms of the formation of the Induction Support Team, the identification of the mentor's responsibilities, the components and processes of the orientation session, and the initiation of the Personal Development Plan.

Ward, B. A. (1987). State and district structures to support initial year of teaching programs. In G. A. Griffin & S. Millis (Eds.), *The first years of teaching: Background papers and a proposal*. Chicago: University of Illinois.

Action in induction programs is necessary in three areas to ensure that beginning teachers find ways to fulfill new roles and demands while acquiring an expanding view of their roles as teachers. First, two types of training must be available: a focus on adjustment to the complex world of teaching, and an emphasis on acquisition of skill, knowledge, and perceptions that exemplify an ideal teacher. Second, institutions involved in the induction process must collaborate to provide implementation of training and support services based on knowledge about effective teaching and to promote teachers' use of this knowledge. Third, clear standards must be developed. The author describes six structures to address these needs. These include mentor teacher, teacher development, schools, school district/university collaboratives, a center for teacher quality, and clear standards for both the initial years of teaching and teaching advancement.

Wildman, T., & Borko, H. (1985). *Beginning teacher's handbook*. Blacksburg, VA: Virginia Polytechnic, College of Education.

By reviewing some of the major patterns of findings in the last 15 years, the authors attempt to sensitize beginning teachers to the usefulness and limitations in using research findings to improve their teaching. The authors view teachers as problemsolvers who are guided by reflective, systematic thinking about teaching and the learning process. They suggest different ways of organizing information, presenting instruction, and managing classrooms.

APPENDIX
GUIDELINES FOR WRITING VIGNETTES

Close-to-the-Classroom Casebooks

These casebooks will provide a way of capturing two kinds of teacher knowledge. One is the knowledge about learning the basics of classroom teaching; this is knowledge to pass on to beginning teachers. The second is the knowledge that experienced teachers have gained working as mentors; this is knowledge to pass on to new mentors.

Cases are used in many professions, both to prepare novices for their new role and to make available and accessible a body of knowledge. Unlike law and medicine, teaching traditionally has not had a case literature. Educators have not had a mechanism to accumulate the wealth of knowledge that teachers possess. As a result, we leave no legacy to those who follow us.

Our first product, *The Mentor Teacher Casebook*, includes vignettes written by mentor teachers about their work with beginning teachers. That book accumulated a set of cases that can be passed on as a legacy to new mentors. The proposed casebook, *The Intern Teacher Casebook**, will generate descriptions of situations and problems that confront trainees in their early years of teaching. Together, the two casebooks can help inform others in developing support programs for new teachers.

What Is a Vignette?

A vignette is a story about a particular event, experience, or relationship. It is a narrative which has a beginning, a middle, and an end. The vignette describes what led up to the event and the consequences that followed the event. To the extent possible, it also describes how the participants in the event were thinking and feeling.

Examples of vignettes for this casebook can be divided into two categories. The first category includes descriptions of classroom events, such as the following:

1. You prepared a lesson during which you wanted to explain a new concept or teach a new skill. The kids didn't understand what you were teaching. Describe the event. How did the pupils respond? What did you do? As you thought about the lesson later that night, perhaps you came up with a new approach. How did it go? Why?

2. Can you remember a situation where you had to teach a lesson or a unit that you didn't know anything about? How did you prepare yourself to teach? What resources did you use? Where did you turn for help? How did you teach the unit, step by step? How did you feel the unit went? If you

were to reteach the unit, what would you do differently?

3. Can you remember a nontraditional activity that you organized that didn't work (e.g., small groups, science laboratory, independent research, creative dramatics)? How did you prepare for it? What different alternatives did you consider for the activity? Describe the instruction as if you were writing a newspaper account or a short story. What would you do differently if you were to reuse the activity?

In the second category are descriptions of interactions or relationships with students, colleagues, or administrators:

1. Have you had individual students or a small group of students that persistently acted out or refused to do work? You tried different things or used someone else's suggestions, but the kids continued to cause problems and drove you up the wall. Or, your new strategies paid off. Tell your story.

2. Have you had any interactions with a mentor teacher, an administrator, or another teacher which made a real difference in your teaching? Alternatively, have you had an interaction that was ineffective or even harmful? Tell your story.

These are just a few examples to help you think about what a vignette would look like. But the most important factor is that the event or relationship about which you write is one that had significance for you and your development as a teacher.

Structure of the Vignette

Opening Statement. In what stage of the Teacher Trainee Program are you? Briefly describe your personal and academic background. Where did you do your undergraduate work? What is your major? What courses did you particularly enjoy? What previous experience have you had with the same age group as your students?

Description of Context. Describe both the size and location of you school and the ethnic and socioeconomic diversity of your students. Are there any handicapped youngsters in your classroom? What are the range of abilities of your students? In what month or season did the event or interaction take place? If you write about an instructional event: What period of the day is the event? Draw a diagram of the classroom in which the vignette occurred. Place the teacher's desk in relation to the students.

* These guidelines were given to the teachers who contributed to this volume to guide the writing of their vignettes.

Now, tell your story with a beginning, a middle, and an end, as if you were writing a newspaper account or a short story. Specifically indicate any place where a mentor teacher, another colleague, or an administrator either provided help or tried to provide help. What were the consequences? When would you have wanted help, but didn't get it?

Write as vivid a picture of the account as you can. But do not worry about your writing. You will have opportunities to revise your vignette. Minimal editing will also be done by Far West Laboratory before the casebook is published.

Choose a vignette within either category:

Description of a Classroom Event. Tell a story about a lesson or unit. When you began your planning, what was your mental image of how the lesson/unit would have gone? If your plans had worked perfectly, how would you have wanted things to go? Describe what occurred. Were there any surprises?

Description of an Interaction. What occurred during the preceeding days, weeks, or months that would help us to understand the interaction? Describe the interaction. What were the outcomes of the interaction? We would be particularly interested in descriptions of interactions with mentor teachers.

—101W

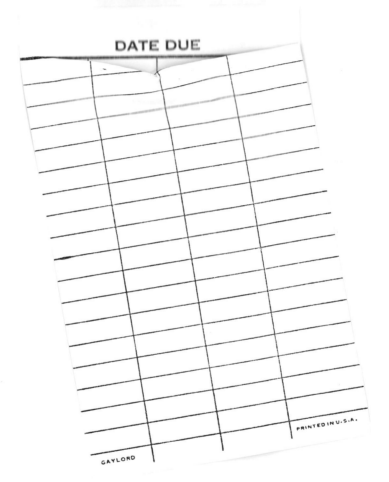

DATE DUE

GAYLORD

PRINTED IN U.S.A.